Making Creative Schedules Work!

in Middle and High Schools

Elliot Y. Merenbloom

Barbara A. Kalina

Foreword by Gordon Cawelti

CORWIN PRESS
A SAGE Publications Company
Thousand Oaks, CA 91320

For information:

Corwin Press
A Sage Publications Company
2455 Teller Road
Thousand Oaks, California 91320
www.corwinpress.com

Sage Publications Ltd.
1 Oliver's Yard
55 City Road
London EC1Y 1SP
United Kingdom

Sage Publications India Pvt. Ltd.
B-42, Panchsheel Enclave
Post Box 4109
New Delhi 110 017 India

Printed in the United States of America

Library of Congress Cataloging-in-Publication Data

Merenbloom, Elliot Y.
Making creative schedules work in middle and high schools/Elliot Y. Merenbloom and Barbara A. Kalina.
       p. cm.
Includes bibliographical references and index.
ISBN-13: 978–1–4129–2424–5 (cloth)
ISBN-13: 978–1–4129–2425–2 (pbk.)
    1. Schedules, School—United States. 2. Educational change—United States.
3. School improvement programs—United States. 4. School management and organization—United States. I. Kalina, Barbara A. II. Title.
LB3032.M47 2007
373.12′42—dc22   2006028717

This book is printed on acid-free paper.

06   07   08   09   10   10   9   8   7   6   5   4   3   2   1

Acquisitions Editor:	Jean Ward
Editorial Assistant:	Jordan Barbakow
Production Editor:	Beth A. Bernstein
Copy Editor:	Halim Dunsky
Typesetter:	C&M Digitals (P) Ltd.
Proofreader:	Word Wise Webb
Indexer:	Rick Hurd
Cover Designer:	Lisa Riley

Making Creative Schedules

Work!

in Middle and High Schools

For Ryan and Benjamin;
Angela, Matthew, Josephine, Elizabeth, George, Marion, August;
and all other grandchildren of the world,
may their legacy be affirmed in a life
of dynamic change

Contents

List of Tables
and Figure

Foreword

Restructuring refers to fundamentally changing the way an organization conducts its "business," be that making cars or educating youth. This book provides insights into perhaps the most powerful tool for restructuring secondary schools by showing how alternative schedules can be put in place that compel better planning by teachers and enable them to provide more in-depth learning experiences for their students. Years ago someone said you have to construct schools to get in the way of bad teaching, and the same can certainly be said for building the daily schedule that provides the basis for teaching and learning activities.

Pressures have been on secondary schools for many years to improve their effectiveness. The symptoms of dysfunction are well known by now to most people even though the symptoms are not present in all schools—low rates of attendance, large gaps in student achievement levels between subgroups in today's diverse student bodies, and a high dropout rate in many schools. The press tends to focus much more on these issues than it does on the accomplishments of schools, which are numerous and noteworthy.

There have been many changes in society that are well known to teachers and administrators but it is often very difficult to figure out what to do about them. The United States continues to have large numbers of immigrants arriving every year, often with limited English skills. Teachers often find it difficult to collaborate with parents in the education process because many students have only one parent at home, if any. The powerful influence of other educative factors in a teenager's life such as television, movies, computers, and technology-based "toys" is often much more compelling than a lecture or other passive learning activities. Parents often find it difficult to get their children involved in traditional family activities because their children find the activities "boring."

One problem in planning to deal with these dysfunctional systems and societal changes is that very often well-meaning politicians make the situation worse by enacting legislation that actually promotes "drill and kill" learning activities. This is much to the dismay of teachers who have lost instructional time for exploratory activities out of the necessity to improve test scores. However, one could argue that we educators asked for it by not coming up with our own aggressive solutions for dealing with low achievement, poor attendance, and bored students.

Now is the time for the profession to provide the school-based leadership required to overcome the weaknesses schools continue to exhibit year after year.

Unless school leaders and teachers want more intrusive legislation with honorable intentions but undesirable side effects, now is the time to restructure their middle and high schools. It is time to implement schedules that will enable teachers to regularly engage in planning learning activities of rich intellectual content aimed at exacting standards. *Too many of today's class periods are of short duration and thus limit extended learning activities and the use of teaching and assessment strategies that must be implemented to ensure mastery of standards on a daily and weekly basis.*

One ought not to underestimate the difficulty of changing a school schedule that has been in place for many years, and the authors have not done so, as seen in the time they devote to explaining reasons why secondary schools must change. They have done this to encourage school leaders to engage teachers in discussions that focus on making the case for change, before leaders attempt to plan specific changes themselves. This reflects the extensive experience and expertise the authors have that qualifies them to discuss the advantages and disadvantages of various schedules along with the specific processes and factors that must be considered in planning for implementation.

Careful attention is given to helping teachers plan to work in teams and begin to function as a learning community. Such a community requires participants to grow professionally and benefit from the experience of their colleagues. Teachers and teams must assume responsibility for achieving results, and until they do we will see more "test and punish" legislation. It is unlikely that restructuring a school can truly be accomplished unless the basic pattern of daily classes provides for extended learning periods and time for teachers to work together in facing the realities of what students are bringing to their classes early in the 21st century.

—Gordon Cawelti
Senior Research Associate
Education Research Service
Arlington, Virginia

Preface

As events in the world move our lives with alarming speed, people struggle to make meaningful change. In education, reform and restructure too often become by-words of one-dimensional efforts to implement structural or strategic change. While the speed of world events cannot be slowed, thoughtful implementation of educational structures and strategies stimulates the change process and transforms reform and restructuring into multidimensional gains for the teaching-learning process.

This process of transformation requires a guide, and those involved must determine the pace. The text of *Making Creative Schedules Work in Middle and High Schools* provides that guide to help educators participate actively in three phases of the restructuring process: organization for the delivery of instruction, small learning communities or teams, and teaching in variable lengths of time. The content draws from Elliot Y. Merenbloom's years of experience as a teacher, school counselor, building administrator, central office director, and full-time consultant. His expertise in scheduling and in the role of scheduling in meeting the needs of today's students has inspired a myriad of schools and districts. In tandem with Elliot's expertise, Barbara A. Kalina brings her experience as a classroom teacher, team leader, department head, member of the Illinois State Board of Education writing assessment team, Association of Illinois Middle-Level Schools board member, and consultant. Through their multiple contacts with teachers, schools, and districts as well as their state and national conference presentations, they have seen first hand the dilemmas that the change process presents. Their observations became the inspiration for this book.

Making Creative Schedules Work in Middle and High Schools provides a valuable resource for those charged with the reorganization of schools to improve student achievement. Through the use of this text, teachers and administrators can create and implement a vision for their schools or districts at a pace that accommodates their needs.

Based upon a review of research and best practices in secondary education, the major features of the text include strategies for building middle and high school schedules, implementing small learning communities, developing collaborative instruction, and helping teachers work effectively within variable-length periods as a provision of the schedule. The content addresses the professional needs of prospective principals and superintendents, school-based administrators interested in effecting change, members of the building leadership team, and teachers who implement the change.

Chapter 1 identifies reasons for restructuring and reorganizing as identified nationally in middle and high schools. Since a variety of reasons exist for schools to reorganize, those responsible for building the schedule should understand what they are trying to create and why.

In Chapter 2, a variety of structural options is introduced. Investigating the models with accompanying lists of benefits and limitations, a faculty committee makes selections that reflect teachers' wishes in light of the needs of the student body.

Chapters 3 and 4 introduce specific models to create the schedule or timetable for the middle and high school grades. Those charged with the task of scheduling can easily implement the step-by-step approach and the concrete models provided.

Chapters 5, 6, and 7 focus on small learning communities or teams. Chapter 5 identifies the role and function of a team: responding to student needs, curriculum integration and delivery, and flexible/creative uses of time. In order to effectively implement the model, the teams or small learning communities need to follow a goal-setting process that reflects the research on change. Chapter 6 focuses on the curricular and instructional aspects of the model while Chapter 7 introduces organizational factors.

Chapter 8 contains a comprehensive study of teaching in extended-time periods. Either on a fixed or variable basis, teachers and/or small learning communities have opportunities to apply these teaching prototypes. Models for a pacing guide, unit development plan, and lesson plan prototype enable the teacher or prospective teacher to implement research on this topic in the context of a daily instructional program.

Chapter 9 synthesizes the research on change and staff development. The thirteen statements at the end of the chapter provide the basis for considering the initiation, development, and refinement of reform in three areas: schedules, small learning communities, and teaching in variable length time periods.

As the reader progresses through the three segments of school reform included in *Making Creative Schedules Work in Middle and High Schools*, the authors hope that a more precise vision of the change process will emerge. They believe that the unique nature of this text will provide the impetus necessary to support changes in structures and strategies that will impact student achievement.

Acknowledgments

O
ur inspiration to write this book started many years ago when we began as classroom teachers. We are especially indebted to Harold J. Wolff, former principal of Rotolo Middle School, Batavia, Illinois, who brought a group of teachers to a workshop sponsored by the National Middle School Association on the topic of team approaches to instruction.

Following that workshop, a series of conversations and letters helped us to realize our common views of the learning process, school organization, and why schools exist. As discussion progressed about these topics, our families and friends reinforced the idea of our collaboration. We felt a need existed for an approachable guide to developing schedules and implementing the strategies necessary to use those schedules effectively through the creation of small learning communities and training models for teaching in extended or variable length time periods.

As we started our research, the guidance and works of others in the field of education and educational research encouraged our efforts: Dr. Anthony Mello, Dr. Robert Marzano, and Dr. Gary Brager. Their personal touch augmented the reinforcement received through the research findings of many in the educational community. Dr. Mello especially encouraged us to include "the necessary linkages" to help the reader see the relationship between school organization, small learning communities, and teaching in variable-time periods. We remain indebted to Jean Ward for her belief in the value of the message of our book and her continued support through the various stages of the manuscript. The patience and coaching of our copy editor, Halim Dunsky, contributed to the refinement of our message.

Inspiration, however, dies without application. Ilene Merenbloom provided our application with her ongoing support and typing of multiple drafts. Without her aid, this text might not have moved beyond the inspiration stage. Both Merenbloom sons, Paul and Alan, contributed their computer expertise and served as sounding boards.

The six Kalina children, assorted spouses, and grandchildren cheered us on with frequent calls from their distant homes. Our spouses, Ilene Merenbloom and Richard Kalina, endured our long hours of drafting and revising by telephone. We are indebted to all of our encouragers and supporters. Like a child in a village, a book takes a myriad of supporters to become a reality.

About the Authors

After thirty-three years of service in the Baltimore County (Maryland) Public Schools, **Elliot Y. Merenbloom** chose to pursue a career as an educational consultant. During his career in that district, Elliot served as a classroom teacher, guidance counselor, assistant principal, principal, Director of Middle School Instruction, and Area Director. This is his fourteenth year as a full-time educational consultant.

A graduate of Towson University and Loyola College of Maryland, his areas of expertise include creative scheduling, teaching strategies for variable-length time periods, restructuring/change process, organizational strategies, staff development, teams/small learning communities, and curriculum implementation.

Elliot authored two books for the National Middle School Association and twelve articles that have been published in various educational journals. The *Middle School Journal* featured an "Interview With Elliot Merenbloom: Reflections on the Principalship," focusing on the importance of the principal in implementing effective schools.

In addition to leading workshops and seminars for the American Association for Development, Silver-Strong and Associates, the Illinois Renewal Institute, the National Association of Secondary School Principals, the National Middle School Association, and the New England League of Middle Schools, Elliot has served as a consultant for school districts in forty-five states as well as Guam; Vienna, Austria; and Vancouver, British Columbia.

Elliot was a consultant for the first European Conference on Middle Level Education. He lectured at the Principals' Center of Harvard University, and provided training under the auspices of The Education Alliance of Brown University.

Barbara A. Kalina completed studies and work as a registered nurse prior to becoming a literature, language arts, social studies teacher. She received her bachelor and master degrees from Mundelein College, Chicago, Illinois, with majors in British literature and philosophy.

After twenty-three years of teaching at Sam Rotolo Middle School of Batavia, Illinois, Barbara retired from the dual world of teaching seventh grade students and offering professional development to the singular world of staff development consultation. During her teaching years, she held a variety of leadership positions, including middle school transition team member, team leader, and Language Arts department chair. Additionally, she served as an adjunct professor teaching courses on middle school philosophy, methods, and curriculum at Benedictine University and National Louis University in Illinois.

Besides the rich experience gained in teaching middle school students, Barbara brings to her consultant work sixteen years of active involvement as member and conference presenter with the Association of Illinois Middle-Level Schools, the National Middle School Association, the Association for Supervision and Curriculum Development, and the Illinois Association for Supervision and Curriculum Development. For twenty years, she served as member, trainer, and assessment developer for various Illinois State Board of Education language arts committees, focusing on reading and writing.

In addition to coauthoring *Making Creative Schedules Work in Middle and High Schools*, she has contributed to the National Association of Elementary School Principals' publication *Middle Matters*.

Based on a strong commitment to research-based strategies, Barbara presents professional development workshops in the areas of literacy, curriculum development, small learning community/team process, teaching in variable-length time periods, and effective utilization of the master schedule. Her workshops feature the active involvement of participants to facilitate the immediate implementation of these strategies.

1

Why Are Schools Reorganizing?

Pick up any newspaper; listen to any radio or television talk show; check the book catalogues clogging our mailboxes. When the focus is education, one theme permeates them all: change. The demands for change seem to challenge the mentality that Dolan (1994), in *Restructuring Our Schools*, calls "system-in-place" (p. 5), the mentality that resists attempts to reform, restructure, or reorganize. Along with Dolan, others caution us to recognize the complexity of a system's interconnections that place obstacles in the path of change (Jackson & Davis, 2000, pp. 27–28; McAdams, 1997; Senge, Cambron-McCabe, Lucas, Smith, Dutton, & Kleiner, 2000, p. 11; Zmuda, Kuklis, & Kline, 2004). Part of this complexity includes the five pressure groups identified by Erickson (2001, pp. 2–10): business and the world of work, state governments, social forces, media, and parents. McAdams suggests five somewhat different factors: "quality of leadership, local politics and governance, state and national politics, organizational characteristics, and change." Within this challenging climate, school districts and educators alike may feel controlled by the tides of change rather than in control of them. In the attempt to navigate the sea of expectations, a danger exists of losing education's true mission: to meet the academic needs of each student by "recreating schools to serve students who will grow up in a post-industrial world" (Senge et al., p. 9).

To fulfill their role and meet the challenges, many secondary schools seek to incorporate the change process as a common and ongoing element of their culture. Through observation and evaluation of their specific needs, successful schools take an inside out, step-by-step approach to change, each step dependent on the implementation of the previous steps (National Association of Secondary School Principals [NASSP], 1996; Zmuda, Kuklis, & Kline, 2004). Some identified school changes include reorganization of time, materials, resources, students, and teachers; new approaches to scheduling; curriculum delivery; and professional collaboration. Impetus for these changes is generated by expectations of community, parents, boards of education, and accreditation agencies. Individually and as part of a school improvement team, teachers along with administrators contribute their voices to the reform process. Through their research of theory, best practices, and classroom initiatives, they can create models for schoolwide adoption.

Today and especially since the reform of the Elementary and Secondary Education Act of 1965, more familiarly known as the No Child Left Behind Act of 2001, laws mandate change. These changes include increased accountability for states, school districts, and schools; greater choice for parents and students, particularly those attending low-performing schools; more flexibility for states and local educational agencies (LEAs) in the use of federal education dollars; and a stronger emphasis on reading, especially for our youngest children. Those laws require schools and districts to demonstrate that adequate yearly progress and the needs of all student populations are being met.

FIFTEEN FACTORS FOR RESTRUCTURING

This chapter identifies fifteen factors for leaders and teachers to consider as they evaluate their purposes and options for the improvement of learning. These options apply to schools that are challenged to improve performance as well as schools that are currently performing well and seeking ways to provide even greater learning opportunities. These factors include the most frequently identified catalysts for change: points that cry out for increased support of students and targeted elements that require restructuring.

Ideally, purposes for reorganizing should be clearly identified throughout the early stages of the restructuring process. Prior to a revision of schedules, curriculum, and models of professional collaboration, leaders and teachers should analyze these topics as they relate to the local setting. The final assessment of the reorganization effort should be based upon reasons that address community needs, not just the schedule, student scores, or a survey. Fifteen factors to guide the decision-making process follow:

1. Respond to student needs.

2. Ease transition from elementary school to middle school.

3. Facilitate transition from middle school to high school.

4. Make effective use of available full-time equivalent (FTE) positions.

5. Increase or decrease the number of periods in the day.

6. Lengthen the instructional module.

7. Address state and national standards.

8. Improve student achievement.

9. Provide remediation.

10. Establish teams, houses, small learning communities, magnets.

11. Move locus of control from management to teacher.

12. Incorporate looping.

13. Provide opportunities for inclusion of special needs students.

14. Group and regroup students for a variety of instructional purposes.

15. Establish advisory programs.

These considerations are numbered for convenient reference but are not presented in order of importance. In fact, multiple purposes for reorganization exist, and many of these reasons are interrelated. School leaders and teachers should look at options for change presented in the following chapters, including schedules, small learning communities, and teaching in variable time periods. They may identify important factors that may be of interest or mandated. At the end of this chapter and each subsequent chapter, a set of questions appears for both leaders and teachers. The process of answering these questions is key to the effective utilization of the book as a tool in restructuring.

Respond to Student Needs

Technically, all schools exist to serve students and to respond to their needs. In actuality, some schools accomplish this task better than others. In essence, the middle school concept arose from a concern about meeting adolescent needs. In the middle of the twentieth century, studies looked more closely at the early adolescent student. Through those studies, researchers found that the needs of these students differed from the needs of the elementary student. Dr. William Alexander and Dr. Donald Eichorn, two of the early pioneers in this effort, wrote extensively about early adolescent students, describing their characteristics and introducing pedagogy designed to meet their needs. Today, the authors of *Breaking Ranks* (NASSP, 1996) and *Breaking Ranks II* (NASSP, 2004) reinforce those findings and extend them into the high school arena. Programs such as freshman academies, advisory programs, magnet experiences, and house plans for Grades 9 to 12 emerge in this response to student needs.

Ease Transition From Elementary School to Middle School

Parents perceive that the elementary school is a safe, secure environment where one classroom teacher is responsible for coordinating the learning experience of one class of students. In *The Handbook of Research in Middle Level Education,* Anfara (2001) reports the study completed by Williamson and Johnston (1998) regarding parental attitudes toward middle level schools. Parents in four communities voiced four major concerns: potential student anonymity within the larger middle school, unclear curriculum content, minimal curriculum rigor, and instruction that did not engage students. Based on these observations, Anfara suggests that the results of the Williamson and

Johnston study may be attributed to community perceptions rather than reality or to inadequately prepared middle school faculty.

Since test scores at the elementary school level are frequently higher than comparable scores in Grades 6–8 (Alspaugh, 1998), parents wish to extend the security and perceived success of elementary school beyond Grade 5 or 6. Consequently, some communities are creating K–8 schools in an effort to keep the student in what they believe to be a safe environment. Many of the K–8 schools, however, lack the comprehensive secondary curriculum, resources, and teachers trained in content areas. This becomes a dilemma.

In a *New York Times* article, Deborah Nussbaum (2004) identifies some of the attitudes for and against middle level schools, noting especially the urban school situations in which truancy and the loss of individual attention play a part. A K–8 advocate, Cheri Pierson Yecke (2006) created a stir in the middle level school community when she questioned the success of middle level education by calling to account its academic rigor. In part, the rebuttal to her charges occurred before the accusation: Felner, Jackson, Kasak, Mulhall, Brand, and Flowers (1997) emphasized that achievement and success in the middle level grades require full implementation of the middle school philosophy and practices rather than the cafeteria selection approach that has too often perpetuated the system-in-place. According to McEwin, Dickinson, and Jenkins (2003), however, the trend to reorganize from middle level schools to K–8 remains limited. Therefore, the burden to provide a safe transition is incumbent upon the middle level school. Overall, decision makers recognize the importance of addressing the specific needs of this unique population, which includes the recognition of developmental needs and academic rigor.

Another related issue appears to be the transition from a self-contained environment to departmentalization. While some middle schools include self-contained fifth- and sixth-grade classes, most middle schools feature interdisciplinary teams. School personnel develop a variety of activities to ease the transition for the student as well as for the parent, activities such as middle level and elementary student visitations, parent-student orientations to the building, and team letters or phone calls. As required by current law (No Child Left Behind), middle level teachers are more often subject matter specialists. They collaborate to deliver the total core curriculum according to the individual needs of their student team. When effective, the team becomes the security for students.

McEwin, Dickinson, and Smith (2004) maintain that middle level schools can carry out their original mission and attain the goals of intellectual and individual development during these early adolescent years. As evidence, they cite the ongoing research completed by Mertens, Flowers, and Mulhall at the Center for Prevention, Research, and Development (CPRD) at the University of Illinois, Champaign (1998, 2001, 2003). In November 2002, Mulhall, Flowers, and Mertens reported the importance of considering and understanding all of the data regarding this age group, not only the standardized achievement score data. By implementing a larger body of disaggregated data, schools and districts are better able to develop intervention methods for immediate action and for program evaluation.

Aware of the challenge before them, today's middle schools are reorganizing to achieve the necessary balance between the security of the elementary-oriented teacher and the subject matter specialization of secondary teachers. In this way, they facilitate the transition of students.

Facilitate Transition From Middle to High School

An equally important transition takes place between middle school and high school. From the inception of the middle school concept, districts assigned ninth grade students to high school campuses. Whereas middle school education attempted to create a different experience for those sixth graders housed in a 6–8 building, ninth graders were given the "standard" high school schedule and often were not successful in that model. Success was measured in terms of grade point average, retention and dropout rates, attendance and tardiness, participation in extracurricular activities as well as suspensions and expulsions.

In the current 9–12 high school model, more developmentally appropriate measures are being used to determine success. High school educators address the transition of students from Grades 8 to 9 by creating academies or small learning communities to deliver the ninth grade curriculum and an advisory component to facilitate the adjustment to Grade 9. High school counselors and administrators meet with their middle level colleagues to learn more about the nature and needs of the rising freshman class. Some districts establish separate freshman schools within the high school structure. To facilitate the adjustment, the advisory component includes study skills, test preparation, conflict resolution, decision making, career development, and communication skills. In the NASSP report *Breaking Ranks* (2004), this advisory component appears as one of the strategies necessary for essential high school reform.

As in the transition from elementary to middle school, ninth grade teachers strive to achieve the proper balance between the security provided by the team or small learning community within the middle school philosophy and the subject matter specialization ultimately needed in Grades 10–12.

Make Effective Use of Available Full-Time Equivalent (FTE) Positions

In many school districts, the superintendent allocates FTEs or a fixed number of personnel to each building principal, who then apportions these positions to each department, team, house, or academy. When a district loses positions because of budget reductions or declining enrollment, when special education or bilingual positions displace regular education positions, or when graduation or state requirements change, adjustments affect the FTE distribution.

Several subtopics further compound the issue of FTE allocation:

- Number of periods in the school day
  - Schools moving from a six- or seven-period day to an eight-period day realize the need for additional staff to offset an increase in average class size and/or average daily pupil loads. Because of reductions in staffing mandated by the district, some schools change to a six-period day.

- Number of periods per day a teacher can teach
  - Beyond the question of the number of periods in the day is the issue of the number of periods in the day a teacher can teach. Districts looking to move to an eight- or nine-period day with contract language limiting a teacher to five teaching periods will recognize the need for more staff when restructuring.

- Allocation of team meeting or department meeting as a non-contact period (that time spent without students)
  - Ideally, teachers should have a team or department meeting as well as a personal planning period. Effective implementation of the middle school concept and small learning communities in the high school requires professional planning meetings during the school day.

- Teacher availability for duties
  - As teachers dedicate time to team and/or department meetings, they may not be available for various duties typically associated with the function of the school. Hard decisions must be made regarding the best use of teachers' non-contact time.

- Average daily pupil load per teacher
  - Boards of Education and union associations work hard to minimize the number of students a teacher sees during a particular day. Revisions of the program of studies, course offerings, or number of periods in the day may have an impact on the average daily pupil load of each teacher.

- Provisions available for teachers to teach extra classes
  - As districts strive to offer magnet as well as remedial programs, the staff available on a contractual basis may not be adequate for the number of sections to be offered. In some districts, teachers can volunteer to teach an extra class and receive a stipend.

Because of the many forces that have an impact on the utilization of available FTEs, decisions on the effective use of available FTEs are critical.

Increase or Decrease the Number of Periods in the Day

In the discussion of the effective use of available FTEs, the number of periods in the school day emerges as a key piece in the saga of school restructuring. Typically, schools are organized into four-, six-, seven-, eight-, or nine-period days. Four-period days are associated with extended or variable time-period instruction.

Generally, the six-, seven-, eight-, or nine-period options present both positive and negative issues. In a six-period day, districts minimize the number of courses a student may take and the number of teachers on staff. In this model, teachers teach five of the six periods. Students receive fewer elective classes and have less opportunity for higher levels of mathematics, science, or foreign language; however, periods approximate sixty minutes in length.

In a seven-period day, greater opportunity exists for electives as well as upper level courses in high school. In many schools, teachers teach five classes and are scheduled for a team meeting as well as a personal planning period. Further, this schedule allows a fuller encore or exploratory program in the middle school. Classes in the seven-period day are 40 to 50 minutes.

Eight- and nine-period models provide greater opportunities for exploratory, elective, or remedial classes. As schools move from a six- or seven-period day to an eight- or nine-period day, more staff positions may be needed if teachers are contracted to teach five classes per day. Without an increase in staff, class sizes increase. Interdisciplinary team teachers may offer a flex or student support period to minimize the increase in staffing. Unless teachers can be assigned six instructional periods or five instructional and one flex/support period, the eight- or nine-period day is less likely to occur with the existing staff. When schools reorganize, restructure, or create small learning communities, the number of periods in the day becomes a crucial factor.

Lengthen the Instructional Module

Discussing the number of periods in the school day is tangential to discussing the length of each instructional module. Before the early 1990s, most secondary schools operated on a seven-, eight-, or nine-period day with periods from 40 to 50 minutes; some schools operated on a six-period day at 60 minutes each. Teachers' schedules were based upon a class meeting of 40 to 50 minutes. Their preservice training, including student teaching, provided this as the norm or another example of system-in-place. Lessons that were not completed in 40 to 50 minutes were completed the next day. The lesson consisted of a drill, warm-up activity, major presentation, guided practice or follow-up, summary, and announcement of homework. Rarely, did teachers think in terms of a series of engagements that provided in-depth learning of a topic within the 40 to 50 minutes.

As early as the late 1960s, middle schools started to experiment with 80–90 minute classes on a flexible basis. When the schedule was so constructed, teachers of the interdisciplinary team had the potential to use extended periods for a variety of instructional purposes. For the most part, however, middle grade lessons remained at the traditional length. O'Neil's 1995 study cited by D. F. Brown in "Flexible Scheduling and Young Adolescent Development" (2001) reported that only 15% of secondary schools attempted this model in the 1960s and 1970s (p. 127).

Circa 1990, at the high school level and later at the middle level, teachers' interest in extended periods expanded, energized by developments in the study of students' cognitive development. As the extended period programs began in Grades 9–12, teachers experimented and ultimately implemented 80- to 90-minute class periods. Although many middle school teachers or teams did not choose to implement formal extended period programs, they experimented with flexible schedules.

As early as 1993, McEwin et al. (2003) conducted a study that indicated the impact of time allocation for high-stakes testing. They discovered that language arts and mathematics received proportionally larger allocations of instructional time (pp. 18–19).

The concept of extended time becomes a factor in what Marzano (2003) calls "opportunity to learn." He illustrates the need for extended time by comparing the amount of content to be taught with the actual amount of instructional time available in a standard 40- to 50-minute class period (pp. 22–34). Besides advocating for extended time, he indicates the need for curriculum reform as well so that teachers know, identify, and teach essential content. Additionally, the fifth cornerstone strategy presented in the NASSP report (2004) includes flexible time frames for classes within which instructional strategies address students' individual learning needs. Consequently, in the process of reorganizing, middle and high schools explore not only the impact of the length of the instructional module as a factor in the learning process but also the impact of varied instructional strategies that occur within that extended time period.

Address State and National Standards

Implementing or aligning with state and national standards impacts the organization or structure of secondary schools. Marzano (2003) raises the issue that the intended curriculum (national, state, and/or district standards) may not necessarily match the implemented curriculum, that content delivered by the teacher (p. 23). To develop a decision-making basis for change, schools and districts must answer these five questions:

1. Do all courses meet state and national standards?

2. Have teachers participated in a review of curriculum?

3. Have teachers received training to develop and implement a curriculum consistent with state and national standards?

4. Does a monitoring system exist to confirm the teaching of all required topics?

5. Do textbook purchases provide staff with resources necessary to meet state and national standards?

Specific questions may be raised at the school level:

Middle School

1. Has adequate time been provided daily for reading, language arts, and mathematics?

2. Are science and social studies courses offered each year? Does the content of these courses meet state and national standards at each grade level?

3. Are there adequate periods in the school day to enable the delivery of all required and elective classes?

4. Are courses offered in the year or semester congruent with testing?

5. Are teachers certified or endorsed for courses they teach?

High School

1. Do the required courses reflect state and national standards?

2. Are teachers certified for courses they teach?

3. Are students able to take required courses and still have opportunity for electives?

4. Are courses offered in the identified testing years?

5. Does the enrollment in electives support teaching positions in those areas? Are more FTEs needed in English, social studies, mathematics, and science and fewer in electives?

The movement toward state and national curriculum standards provided an impetus for school reform. This reform raises organizational as well as instructional issues.

Improve Student Achievement

A reason for reorganization is to improve student achievement. Multiple studies and reports cite gaps among various groups of students considered by socioeconomic status, nationality, and gender. Some of those studies and reports appear in the November 2004 special issue of *Educational Leadership*, "Closing Achievement Gaps," and reinforce the causal complexity of the achievement gap. The journal addresses the impact of some of the ingredients of that complexity, reporting data analysis conducted to determine where and why the gaps appear. Causal factors identified include child-rearing practices, testing practices and preparation, socioeconomic status of parents and school districts, and child health.

These gaps raise issues for the community at large as well as the academic community. In part, the issues arise from the publishing of school and district scores that become a perceived beacon of educational success in the eyes of the public. Government officials, taxpayers, and parents want a quantifiable way to measure the effectiveness of the educational process. The publishing of scores in local newspapers causes the community to make judgments regarding the administration and teaching staff. When progress is not realized, these parties demand answers, a plan for improvement, and, ultimately, new leadership. If scores remain low, state agencies take over the schools.

In an effort to raise test scores, pressure exists for homogeneous grouping. McEwin et al. (2003) hypothesize that high-stakes testing may be the basis to move to more rigid tracking practices in middle level schools (p. 62). In high school, prerequisites for certain courses virtually ensure the existence of homogeneous classes.

Another implication of the analysis of student performance concerns the use of extended periods. Overall, due to the difficulty of gaining empirical evidence, the overt results do not show with certainty whether the reallocation of time has improved student achievement (McEwin et al., 2003, p. 62). On the other hand, when Marzano introduces the five school-level factors that affect student achievement, he cites the Scheerens and Bosker 1997 research studies that indicate the importance of time in content coverage and opportunity to learn (Marzano, 2003). The research does suggest, however, that more opportunity exists in extended time periods for teachers to use strategies identified by Marzano to raise student achievement and to implement the intended curriculum. This research reinforces the importance of time for learning emphasized by learning and brain theorists in works such as Bransford, Brown, and Cocking (2000) and Sousa (2006).

Regarding the importance or relevance of testing to determine student achievement, Arhar (2003) cites the National Forum to Accelerate Middle Grades Reform (2002). The Forum's high-stakes testing policy reaffirms its position on the importance of meeting student needs: "no single test should ever be the sole determinant of a young adolescent's academic future." Rather, the emphasis should be placed on standards and assessments that "lead to high expectations, foster quality instruction, and support higher levels of learning for every student" (McEwin et al., 2003, p. 64).

To accommodate student needs in light of high-stakes testing, districts are actively involved in curriculum revision. Many districts have revised curriculum to be consistent with what is tested. Teachers work hard to disaggregate data to better identify the extent to which curriculum is aligned with standards. Effective small learning community meeting time focuses on the analysis of data and the collaborative design of pedagogy consistent with the data.

Schools restructure in an effort to improve student achievement. As curriculum is aligned with tests, teachers must identify students' strengths and needs through available data. Teams of teachers need a disaggregated picture of a student's profile to provide integrated instruction geared to student progress. Learning requires a balanced relationship featuring curriculum, instruction, assessment, and school organization.

Provide Remediation

Some schools reorganize to offer or require remediation courses for students who have not succeeded on local, state, or national assessments. Other schools have added an additional period in the school day to allow students to participate in both remedial courses and electives.

Because of the focus on remediation courses, staff for elective classes has been reduced, class size in elective courses has increased, and elective courses with low enrollment have been dropped. Consequently, schedules and staffing patterns have changed. Further, curriculum has been purchased or developed to support the remediation. Although schools and districts struggle to find the proper balance between remedial, elective, and exploratory courses, they cannot ignore the fallout of high-stakes testing. As a result of this focus on remediation, the culture of schools may be changing.

Establish Houses/Small Learning Communities/Magnets

Restructuring plans include the creation of cohorts of teachers who work together to address student needs, work to improve student achievement, integrate curriculum, share successes with appropriate teaching strategies for the targeted population, and make decisions about the nature of the instructional module.

In the process of becoming middle schools, interdisciplinary teams became a part of the schedule. In some cases, these teams had maximum opportunities for control over time; in other cases, teams had limited opportunities for flexibility. In both formats, team meetings were an integral part of the prototype.

As high school faculties have become more aware of the needs of adolescents, they have created small learning communities (SLCs) in conjunction with magnet themes or academies such as arts and sciences, health careers, technology, performing arts, or visual arts. The successful implementation of the various small learning communities requires administrators, teachers, and community members to provide input and fulfill their roles as practitioners of systems thinking, as discussed by Dolan (1994) and others. These programs are being created at an ever-increasing rate to raise performance, grade point average (GPA), and promotion rates of ninth graders. SLC faculties typically consist of English, social studies, mathematics, and science teachers, as well as representatives of specialty areas (Allen, R., 2002; NASSP, 2004).

The cohort group helps students with the transition to high school and focuses on skills that are integral to student success. Collaboratively, teachers provide an integrated curriculum and conduct parent conferences as needed. In one example of meeting student needs in a large high school, Rick Allen reports Evanston Township High School's solution in *Educational Leadership* (2002). By creating home bases, this school seeks to overcome the anonymity experienced by many students in a large high school. The same teacher meets with the same group of students over the four-year high school experience. One teacher explains, "If you don't have a personal relationship with students, you can't ask questions. We know an awful lot about them by the time they're seniors" (p. 38). Evanston's process fulfills the requisite for each student to have an adult advocate as cited in *Breaking Ranks* (NASSP, 1996).

As part of the restructuring effort, the master schedule should be designed to maximize opportunities for flexibility. The key to establish flexibility requires the same teachers to work with the same students during the same periods of the day. These teachers should be scheduled for a common planning time and trained to implement the collaborative process. As addressed in a conversation with Dennis Sparks, Executive Director, National Staff Development Council, and reported in *Breaking Ranks II*, a common meeting time encourages a professional bond with other teachers. Sparks maintains that daily interactions among teachers are "one of the most powerful yet underused sources of professional development and instructional improvement" (NASSP, 2004, p. 45). At the high school level, these cohorts should be placed in the master schedule early in the process as an initial priority. A major consideration in Grades 9 through 12 is to move from a departmentalized approach in all grades to an interdisciplinary model that better serves students.

Creating or modifying schedules for houses, magnets, and small learning communities typifies the restructuring effort. Concurrently, in order to maximize the impact of the restructuring process, classroom practice needs to change. In support of this need, Noguera (2004) cites the Fullan and Miles

(1992) study: If organizational changes are not accompanied by intense focus on other areas, especially in instruction, effective change will not occur. Without a more systemic approach, the schedule alone cannot bring the desired outcomes.

Move Locus of Control
From Management to Teacher

Beyond site-based decision making (central office vs. local school), locus of control looks at the broader spectrum of decision making. The continuum of control begins with the district office and moves through the principal to the small learning community and, ultimately, to the classroom teacher. The effectiveness of more teacher control appeared in a longitudinal study of middle school teaming initiatives completed by the University of Illinois Center for Prevention Research and Development. The research affirms the impact of strong, effective teams on student success (Felner et al., 1997). Part of the effectiveness of these teams comes from their empowerment to make decisions. Other reports (Jackson & Davis, 2000; NASSP, 2004) indicate the correlation between the various levels of decision making regarding time, pedagogy, and student success.

A district's policy on locus of control can be achieved by working through the following questions:

District Office

1. What decisions regarding instruction does the superintendent make?

2. What is the basis of the superintendent's decisions or recommendations?

3. Are all decisions subject to the negotiation process? Why or why not?

4. How do teachers demonstrate their response to district office decisions?

5. Are all middle and high schools in a district organized similarly?

Principal

1. Is the principal able to make decisions within the guidelines of the superintendent and other district office personnel?

2. Under what conditions is the principal able to make decisions independently?

3. Does the principal empower teams, departments, and/or teachers to make decisions independently?

Small Learning Communities

1. What training is available to small learning communities to help them make decisions?

2. What types of decisions do these subgroups make?

3. What accountability exists? To whom?

Classroom Teacher

1. What decisions can a teacher make regarding curriculum and instruction?

2. How do teachers gain the background to make decisions regarding curriculum and instruction?

3. How are teachers empowered to utilize best practices and research in instruction on a daily basis?

As the locus of control moves from the superintendent to the principal to the small learning community to the teacher, it becomes more likely that students receive focused, needed benefits. To maintain the locus of control leadership approach, a shared vision and collaboration among all of the political entities need to occur (Lipsitz, Mizell, Jackson, & Austin, 1997). Further, due to personnel changes, it becomes necessary to develop leadership at the various levels. Administrators who develop a shared system of governance and distribute leadership set the stage for smooth transitions when they and key teachers leave the school or district. Lambert (2005) refers to this process as "high leadership capacity" (p. 64). Essentially, districts and schools implement the practice of locus of control in an effort to improve student achievement.

Incorporate Looping

Looping allows teachers to move with students for two or more consecutive years in the same subject. Although teachers may fear leaving their areas of comfort, looping can be implemented smoothly. Few assignments need to change for the first year of the project. In some cases, a major change may be needed to modify teacher assignments in order to create teaching teams. Teachers who loop become familiar with the standards, common instructional goals, and opportunities for differentiation in each curricular area.

Vicki Mogil, principal of Emerson Middle School in Niles, Illinois, reveals (personal communication, 2005) that her teachers and administrators "love the loop." She credits looping with creating an advocacy for students, saving exit and entrance time from seventh to eighth grade, keeping teachers fresh in their subject areas, and providing curriculum continuity. She ends her comments with "Kids really feel they have a home."

Provide Opportunities for Inclusion of Special Needs Students

In response to federal and state directives, secondary schools appear to be wrestling with appropriate ways to provide the least restrictive environment or the opportunity for inclusion. Restructuring efforts require the expansion and/or refinement of programs for special needs students. Hines (2001) suggests that the middle school environment lends itself to inclusive practice because of the existence of interdisciplinary teaching teams. These teams often have more experience in coteaching and can utilize that experience when teaching with a colleague proficient in adaptations or special needs.

Larger high schools can provide a continuum of services for special needs students to ensure the least restrictive environment. To establish the continuity, students can be initially placed as needed and adjusted along the slide or continuum when appropriate as noted in Table 1.1.

Table 1.1   High School Special Education Slide or Continuum Model

English Department	Course Number	Explanation
Ms. Smith	1005–01	English 10 Gifted
Mr. Albion	1000–01	English 10 Standard—No Support
Ms. Greenwood	1009–01	English 10 Standard with Support
Mr. Johavi		Special Education teacher available to support Ms. Greenwood
Mr. Greer	9100–01	English 10 Replacement for special education students with learning disabilities as described in IEP
Mrs. Miller	9900–01	Self-contained Special Education English 10

A student not needing support is with Ms. Smith or Mr. Albion. The majority of the special needs students, however, are in Ms. Greenwood's class with support from Mr. Johavi. Mr. Greer works with learning-disabled students whose Individual Education Programs (IEPs) call for a small class taught by a special education teacher. Mrs. Miller's class houses students who are self-contained, perhaps for English, social studies, mathematics, or science.

Middle and high schools are reorganizing to provide the least restrictive environment for special needs students. Toward this goal, the schedule complements differentiation of instruction and unique teaching strategies for this population.

Group and Regroup Students for a Variety of Instructional Purposes

The traditional junior high school schedule featured a group of 25–32 students who traveled together during the day. The traveling section was called 7A, 8D, or 9G. Theoretically, administrators attempted to create classes based on standardized test scores, teacher recommendation, and/or parent request.

In some schools, the move toward heterogeneous grouping altered this pattern. On the other hand, high school students are individually scheduled based on student requests. Some high school courses are leveled; others are grouped heterogeneously.

Recently, the middle school has moved toward more individualized scheduling. Although a cohort of students, numbering 125 to 140, may be assigned to a group of core teachers for academic subjects, these students may be grouped and regrouped during the course of the five core periods. Williamson and Johnston (1998) emphasize the importance of fitting the educational practice to the needs of the students rather than staying within a rigid grouping. By grouping and regrouping within the academic block, both high- and low-achieving students' needs can be met. Throughout the remainder of the day, students move to art, music, physical education, technology, and family and consumer sciences.

When schedules facilitate grouping and regrouping, teachers have opportunities to reorder and address the individual needs of students. Regrouping examples include the following:

Middle School

- Students needing remediation may be placed in the class that houses special education students in the inclusion program.
- Cross-team regrouping may permit gifted students to be spread over two or more teams.
- In physical education, students can choose certain activities based on their interests.
- Students can be grouped and regrouped in a specific class according to instructional needs, strategies, and learning styles.

High School

- Students are individually scheduled for gifted, remedial, and/or regular program classes throughout the day.
- Two teachers of mathematics or foreign language classes can group and regroup students based upon learning styles and performance on diagnostic pretests.
- Teachers committed to group work or cooperative learning can continually place students in a variety of settings and monitor student performance.
- A course could be organized on a self-pacing curriculum.

Individual teachers can regroup within their classrooms to provide differentiated instruction. Tomlinson's (1999) three-part model of content, process, and product for differentiated instruction encourages this type of organization. By having different groups within a classroom, a teacher can focus on the same concept with the entire class but vary the level of complexity of the process or product.

Establish Advisory Programs

In keeping with the Carnegie Task Force's report on adolescent development, *Turning Points* (Task Force on Education of Young Adolescents, 1989), an essential element of the original middle school concept was the advisory component. Advisory time provides the student with a significant adult who provides support and direction (Jackson & Davis, 2000). A teacher's advisory assignment exists in addition to subject area responsibilities. Daily or at least weekly, teachers are scheduled with a group of 15 to 20 students for a program called advisory, homebase, advisor-advisee, or group guidance. Topics typically include conflict resolution, decision making, understanding self and others, communication skills, loyalty, responsibility, and character education. In addition, students select topics to be discussed. When needed, teachers talk individually with students who have questions or concerns.

Anfara and Brown's (2001) discussion of the advisor-advisee program cites Alexander and George (1981) who determined not only that the program benefits students but that effective teachers need and want an opportunity to know at least some of their students in a more meaningful way. Further, in the NASSP publication (2000), *Breaking Ranks: Changing an American Institution*, the researchers advocate that each high school student should have a Personal Adult Advocate similar to the middle school model.

In either scenario, advisory programs impact the schedule. In some cases, advisory is embedded in content area instruction or a magnet program; in others, advisory is a period segment or a full period. At the high school level, interest continues to surface for advisory, freshman seminar, and other student support experiences. In the high school experience, topics include the following:

- social-emotional issues of students in Grades 9–12

- moral development, values, and issues of students in Grades 9–12

- study skills

- career development theory

- career pathways

- school-to-work programs and experiences

- college admissions process

- transition from middle school to high school as well as from high school to college or the world of work

Although advisory is a key element of the secondary curriculum, it is one that is difficult to implement.

SUMMARY

The first step in the reorganization or restructuring process is to identify reason(s) for change. The fifteen factors can be viewed both as reasons for change and as models for change. In all cases, the reason needs to support the focus for change: improving student achievement and meeting student needs. One of these factors, establishing teams, houses, small learning communities, or magnets, might be examined as an option for schools that want to integrate the learning experience and improve student achievement.

A Guide for Collaborative Conversations

To set the stage for further discussion of the fifteen restructuring factors, the following questions should be considered:

Leader Questions

1. Which reasons or topics are of greatest concern?

2. To what extent will restructuring impact student achievement?

3. How do we confirm or validate the reasons for our school or district?

4. What, if any, is the relationship among the reasons selected?

5. What data do we need to move to the next step?

6. How do we arrange for teacher, team, and department conversation?

7. To what extent will restructuring impact teacher accountability?

Teacher Questions

1. From an instructional perspective, which are the major reasons for restructuring?

2. How will restructuring impact curriculum and instruction?

3. How will teachers work in the new organization?

4. How will these changes impact student performance? How will this be measured?

5. What responsibility or accountability exists for teachers in the restructuring process?

2

Structural Options

By processing the content and questions of Chapter 1, the restructuring committee identifies reasons for rethinking the master schedule. The fifteen factors presented in Chapter 1 assist in the analysis of the options or organizational plans in Chapter 2. During the study of Chapter 2, participants will have the opportunity to connect the reasons for restructuring identified in Chapter 1 with the choices presented in this chapter. The charts in Tables 2.1 and 2.2 will guide the process.

Because these options are not mutually exclusive, schedules of middle or high schools may include two or more of these models. While some schools move toward extended periods on a fixed or variable basis, others move away from extended periods for at least some courses. For each option, this chapter contains a definition; reasons for utilization; examples of team, teacher, and student schedules; uses in conjunction with other structural options; and benefits and limitations.

As in Chapter 1, questions for leaders and teachers are offered at the conclusion of the chapter. Initially, the focus of the questions should be for a better understanding of each option: the meaning and possible application of an option for a school, district, or cohort of students. Ultimately, the dialogue created by the questions should facilitate the creation of a comprehensive plan for the schedule that includes chosen options and student benefits.

CHOICES FOR CREATING A MASTER PLAN

Day 1/Day 2 Models

Definition: Middle and high schools have implemented a day 1/day 2 model to set the stage for extended time-period instruction. The schedule is constructed as an eight-period day plus lunch. Lunch can be as short as 20 to 30 minutes or as long as 40 to 50 minutes.

Table 2.1   Reasons for Restructuring or Revising Master Schedule

		School	District
1.	Respond to student needs		
2.	Ease transition from elementary to middle school		
3.	Facilitate transition from middle to high school		
4.	Make effective use of available full-time equivalent (FTE) positions		
5.	Increase or decrease the number of periods in the day		
6.	Lengthen the instructional module		
7.	Address state and national standards		
8.	Improve student achievement		
9.	Provide remediation		
10.	Establish houses, small learning communities, magnets		
11.	Move locus of control from management to teacher		
12.	Incorporate looping		
13.	Provide opportunities for inclusion of special needs students		
14.	Group and regroup students for a variety of instructional purposes		
15.	Establish advisory programs		

Table 2.2   Structural Choices Available

		School	District
1.	Day 1/Day 2		
2.	Semester 1/Semester 2		
3.	Interdisciplinary Team-Maximum Flexibility		
4.	Interdisciplinary Team-Limited Flexibility		
5.	Interdisciplinary Team-Encore or Exploratory program		
6.	Combination Team		
7.	Single Subject Team		
8.	Rotational		

On some days, the entire school can have eight periods at approximately 40 to 45 minutes each. On other days, only periods one to four will meet for 80 to 90 minutes or only periods five to eight for 80 to 90 minutes. One bell schedule is needed for an eight-period day; another bell schedule is needed for days with extended periods. Because of shared staff, some schools are unable to have both eight-period days as well as extended-period days.

In the design of the schedule, teachers receive one non-contact period during periods one to four and one non-contact period during periods five to eight. In this way, a teacher will not teach all four periods on either of the extended-period days. Most teachers have one extended period as a non-contact period in addition to the lunch module. Optimally, teachers involved in small learning communities divide the non-contact time into a team meeting and personal planning period.

Utilization: Middle schools choose day 1/day 2 to reduce the time spent in hallways at the change of class. Besides providing an opportunity to manage student movement, this schedule offers the opportunity to implement different forms of instruction. Although research does not exist to support the positive impact of scheduling alone on student achievement, it does suggest student achievement improves when teachers use pedagogy appropriate for extended periods (Marzano, 2003). In 80- to 90-minute classes, more opportunity exists for active engagement in the learning process. In extended periods, teachers are better able to implement the research on learning styles, multiple intelligences, and differentiation.

This model represents a compromise between the opportunity for extended periods and student readiness for maximum achievement on state and national examinations scheduled throughout the year.

Another benefit of the day 1/day 2 model provides teachers of art, music, technology, world languages, family and consumer sciences, physical education/health, and/or business opportunities for extended periods on a fixed or variable basis. On a fixed basis in middle or high school, the entire school operates on a day 1/day 2 schedule. A variable approach is available to middle school core or exploratory teachers to choose day 1/day 2 variations when desired.

In creating a day 1/day 2 schedule, a specific format as illustrated in table 2.3 is needed. This prototype contains eight periods with a clear delineation separating periods one to four from five to eight. Based upon the teachers' contract, a teacher should have at least one non-contact period during periods one to four and one non-contact period during periods five to eight. Schools utilizing a small learning communities model can schedule team meetings during that non-contact time.

Table 2.3 represents a basic prototype or format for creating a high school schedule on a day 1/day 2 basis. Usually, the schedule organization occurs by department unless ninth grade teams or academies exist. In an actual schedule, course numbers (i.e., 1703) and section numbers (i.e., 01) would replace English 10-01.

Tables 2.4 and 2.5 exemplify a student schedule and a teacher schedule using the day 1/day 2 model.

Table 2.3   High School Teacher Schedule

		Day 1				Day 2			
		1	2	3	4	5	6	7	8
1	Mrs. Jabar	10-01	10-02	X	Journalism I-01	10-03	Honors 11-01	Honors 11-02	X
2	Mr. Toor	AP 12-01	X	AP 12-02	11-01	11-02	X	11-03	Yearbook-01
3	Mr. Lipsitz	9-01	9-02	9-03	X	Drama I-01	X	Honors 9-01	9-04
4	Ms. Jackson	Honors 11-01	Honors 11-02	12-01	X	X	12-02	Speech-01	Speech-02

Table 2.4   High School Student Schedule

	Day 1		Day 2
1	English 10	5	Algebra II
2	World History	6	Band
	Lunch		Lunch
3	Art	7	Technology
4	French II	8	Chemistry

Table 2.5   High School Student Schedule

	Day 1		Day 2
1	English 10-01	5	Drama II-02
2	English 10-02	6	Prep
	Lunch		Lunch
3	Prep	7	English 10-03
4	Drama II-01	8	English 10-04

Table 2.4 represents a typical high school student on a day 1/day 2 schedule. The student is enrolled in eight courses. Lunch is scheduled before reporting to the module 3 and module 7 classes.

The teacher in Table 2.5 meets a total of 6 sections on alternate days throughout the year. The teacher is responsible for four sections of English 10 and two sections of Drama II.

In middle schools, the master schedule is usually written on a team basis. In Table 2.6, team 7A has one teacher of English, social studies, mathematics,

Table 2.6   Middle School Team Schedule

	Day 1				Day 2			
	1	2	3	4	5	6	7	8
English	01	TM/Plan	02	03	04	TM/Plan	05	Flex/Advisory
Social Studies	01	TM/Plan	02	03	04	TM/Plan	05	Flex/Advisory
Math	Algebra 01	TM/Plan	Algebra 02	Pre-Algebra 01	Pre-Algebra 02	TM/Plan	Pre-Algebra 03	Flex/Advisory
Science	01	TM/Plan	02	03	04	TM/Plan	05	Flex/Advisory
Technology/Art	01	TM/Plan	02	03	04	TM/Plan	05	Flex/Advisory
Special Education	Replacement English	TM/Plan	In-Class Support	Replacement Math	In-Class Support	TM/Plan	In-Class Support	Flex/Advisory

science, and special education for the year. A technology teacher is on the team for one semester; an art teacher is on the team the other semester. Classes in English, social studies, science, technology, and art are grouped heterogeneously. Levels in mathematics as well as requirements of the IEP will impact the distribution of students throughout the core periods.

Tables 2.7 and 2.8 demonstrate a student schedule and a teacher schedule using the day 1/day 2 model at the middle school level.

Table 2.7 represents a schedule for one student on the interdisciplinary team. The student is enrolled in English, social studies, French II, Mathematics 8, Science 8, and physical education for the entire year. These classes meet on alternate days. On day 1, period 3, for each quarter of the school year, the

Table 2.7   Middle School Student Schedule

	Day 1		Day 2
1	English 8	5	Mathematics 8
2	Social Studies 8	6	Science 8
	Lunch		Lunch
3	Art/Music/Technology/Family and Consumer Sciences (quarter rotations)	7	Physical Education
4	French II	8	Flex Period/advisory; band and chorus are pull-out programs

student enrolls in one of the exploratory courses. On day 2, period 8, students have a flex period. At this time, band or chorus rehearsal can be held or a student can see a teacher for assistance.

Table 2.8   Middle School Teacher Schedule

	Day 1		Day 2
1	English 8–01	5	English 8–03
2	G/T English 8–01	6	English 8–04
	Lunch		Lunch
3	Team Meeting/ Personal Planning	7	Team Meeting/ Personal Planning
4	English 8–02	8	Flex Period/Advisory

As a member of an interdisciplinary team, the teacher in Table 2.8 has five sections of English 8. Four sections are grouped heterogeneously; one section is designated gifted and talented. In addition to lunch, the teacher has a team meeting for forty minutes and a personal planning period for 40 minutes. During the flex period, the teacher can work with students as needed or conduct an advisory program.

Table 2.9   Day 1/Day 2: Benefits and Limitations

Benefits	Limitations
• Teachers are inclined to utilize a greater number of teaching strategies in this model, especially on days with extended periods. • With the option of 8-period days, teachers feel more comfortable moving to extended periods. The comfort may be more evident when the team makes decisions about time utilization. • The A (all 8 periods), B (periods 1–4), C (periods 5–8) model guarantees at least one all 8-period day per week if the faculty so desires. • This model provides an easier adjustment for transfer students at the high school level. • Advanced Placement and end-of-year exams are accommodated in the day 1/ day 2 model.	• High school students are still enrolled in a full 8-period schedule. • Teachers do not receive a reduction in their pupil loads. In fact, when schools move from 7- to 8-period days, teachers may receive another class to teach. The flex period minimizes the impact. • Curriculum support and professional development are essential for extended period instruction.

Semester 1/Semester 2 Models

Definition: Known as four by four or semester 1/semester 2, this model also provides extended time periods. In this case, a student has four courses per semester at 80 to 90 minutes each. As in day 1/day 2, the schedule is constructed as an eight-period day plus a lunch module of 20 to 40 minutes for students as well as teachers. Periods one to four become semester 1; periods five to eight become semester 2. Teachers receive one non-contact period during modules one to four and one non-contact period during modules five to eight.

Students enroll in four courses in semester one and four different courses in semester two. Exceptions can be made for courses such as band, choir, orchestra, newspaper, and yearbook. These courses can be offered 45 minutes daily both semesters. Due to state and national testing, some high schools are experimenting with mathematics courses for 45 minutes or 90 minutes daily for the year.

Middle schools rarely organize on the pure high school version of semester 1/semester 2. Instead, they have moved to 90 minutes of instruction daily for reading/language arts and/or mathematics for the year. In some cases, social studies is offered for 90 minutes daily one semester, and science is offered 90 minutes daily the other semester.

The semester 1/semester 2 format increases the possibility that each student might have a Personal Adult Advocate as recommended in *Breaking Ranks* (NASSP, 1996). The format of fewer classes allows the student to spend more time with a specific teacher, creating an environment in which a supportive relationship can develop.

Utilization: Through semester 1/semester 2, high schools attempt to provide extended time periods, reduce the number of courses a student takes at a time, and reduce the average daily pupil loads of teachers per semester. Again, both middle school and high school teachers are able to develop scaffolded lessons that incorporate learning styles, multiple intelligences, and differentiation in these extended periods. The additional, non-fragmented time reinforces brain-based research: Learning cannot be rushed and requires time to complete the necessary reflection and processing to increase student learning (Bransford, Brown, & Cocking, 2000). Teachers of encore, exploratory, and/or elective courses have the opportunity for extended periods in the variations of semester 1/semester 2.

The prototype in Table 2.10 allows the creation of a high school schedule designed for a semester 1/semester 2 program. Periods one to four become semester 1; periods five to eight become semester 2.

Tables 2.11 and 2.12 provide examples of a student schedule and a teacher schedule, using the semester 1/semester 2 model at the high school level.

The student in Table 2.11 is enrolled in chemistry, algebra, and English 11 for 80 to 90 minutes in semester 1 and physics, French II, and U.S. history for 80 to 90 minutes in semester 2. Band and physical education are skinnies or yearlong classes at 40 to 45 minutes each day. A skinny is generally 50% of the extended period.

The physics teacher in Table 2.12 teaches three sections (01, 02, 03) in the first semester and an additional three sections (04, 05, 06) during the second semester.

Table 2.10   High School Prototype: Portion of Social Studies Department Schedule

	Semester 1				Semester 2			
	1	2	3	4	5	6	7	8
Mrs. Ojibway	10-01	10-02	10-03	X	10-04	10-05	X	10-06
Mr. Garland	Honors US-01	US-01	X	US-02	Honors US-02	US-03	US-04	X
Ms. Wynn	Gov-01	X	Gov-02	Gov-03	Gov-04	X	Honors Gov-01	Honors Gov-02
Ms. Gonzalez	X	SS 9-01	SS 9-02	Honors SS 9-01	X	Honors SS 9-02	SS 9-03	SS 9-04

Table 2.11   High School Student Schedule

	Semester 1		Semester 2
1	Chemistry	1	Physics
2	Algebra	2	French II
3 A	Physical Education	3 A	Physical Education
3 B	Band	3 B	Band
3 C	Lunch	3 C	Lunch
4	English 11	4	U.S. History

Table 2.12   High School Teacher Schedule

	Semester 1		Semester 2
1	Physics 01	1	Physics 04
2	Physics 02	2	Physics 05
3 A	Prep	3 A	Prep
3 B	Prep	3 B	Prep
3 C	Lunch	3 C	Lunch
4	Physics 03	4	Physics 06

Some schools utilize variations of semester 1/semester 2 within a traditional schedule for students who had a poor experience in their first year of high school. Students who failed several ninth grade courses have an opportunity for credit recovery by repeating English 9 in the first semester (two periods per day) and moving on to English 10 in the second semester (two periods per day) with

Table 2.13   Student Schedule: Credit Recovery Program

1	English 9 and English 10
2	
3	Chorus
4	Algebra I and Algebra II
5	
6	Social Studies 10
7	Physical Education: Monday, Tuesday, Wednesday, Thursday; Physical Science Lab: Friday
8	Physical Science

the same teacher. As illustrated in Table 2.13, this process could be implemented with several courses, even in a traditional eight-period day schedule. Ideally, the student in the example could have junior status in a timely fashion.

In a credit recovery program illustrated in Table 2.13, a student who failed English 9 and algebra in the freshman year can repeat English 9 and Algebra I in the first semester and move into English 10 and Algebra II in the same periods with the same teachers in the second semester. These classes are scheduled for 90 minutes. Other classes are scheduled for 45 minutes: chorus, Social Studies 10, the classroom and lab portions of physical science, and physical education.

Semester 1/semester 2 models have been used extensively in the high school. For the most part, they have been used on a schoolwide basis. In a limited number of cases, a variation of the semestering model is used to implement the credit recovery program. It is intended to facilitate the transition of students who experience difficulty in Grade 9 and want to graduate with their peer group.

Similarly, a variation of semester 1/semester 2 can be used in middle school to provide opportunities for extended time periods on a fixed basis or to serve as a transition from elementary to middle school. For example, a student may have 90 minutes of reading/language arts and 90 minutes of mathematics every day of the school year instead of just one semester. Middle schools use these variations in a two-teacher team as well as a six-teacher team format. In both cases, the goal is to facilitate the transition of students from elementary to middle school by reducing the number of teachers with whom the student needs to identify and by providing a climate for support. Further, the extended time allows teachers to implement strategies designed to raise student achievement.

Tables 2.14 and 2.15 illustrate prototypes for two- and six-teacher interdisciplinary teams. The two-teacher team prototype includes the following features:

- Teacher 1 is responsible for reading/language arts and social studies.
- Teacher 2 is responsible for mathematics and science.
- The student receives 90 minutes of instruction daily in reading/language arts and mathematics.

Table 2.14   Middle School Two-Teacher Team

	Teacher 1		Teacher 2
1	Reading/Language Arts-01	1	Mathematics-02
2	Reading/Language Arts-02	2	Mathematics-01
3	Team Meeting/Personal Prep	3	Team Meeting/Personal Prep
4 A	Social Studies-01	4 A	Science-02
4 B	Social Studies-02	4 B	Science-01

Table 2.15   Middle School Six-Teacher Team

	1	2	3	4	5	6	7	8
Reading/Language Arts-01	01	02	TM/P	03	01	02	TM/P	03
Mathematics-01	03	01	TM/P	02	03	01	TM/P	02
Social Studies	02/05	03/06	TM/P	01/04	02/05	03/06	TM/P	01/04
Science	05/02	06/03	TM/P	04/01	05/02	06/03	TM/P	04/01
Reading/Language Arts-02	04	05	TM/P	06	04	05	TM/P	06
Mathematics-02	06	04	TM/P	05	06	04	TM/P	05

- The student could receive 45 minutes of social studies and science daily or 90 minutes of each course on an alternate day basis.
- The students participate in encore or exploratory courses in module 3.

Ideally, teachers will be certified in both content areas. As another alternative, districts that are more concerned about licensure and highly qualified teachers are examining the six-teacher team model. In this scenario, students participate in reading/language arts and mathematics for 90 minutes every day of the school year. Social studies and science can meet either daily for 45 minutes or 90 minutes on alternate days or alternate semesters. Perhaps of greatest importance, each teacher is licensed in one content area.

Features of the six-teacher team presented in Table 2.15 include the following:

- Students have teachers 01 for reading/language arts and mathematics or teachers 02 for reading/language arts and mathematics.
- Social studies and science teachers have larger pupil loads because they teach 150 students over the course of the year.
- Reading/language arts and mathematics teachers can regroup students.
- Students participate in encore or exploratory courses in modules 3 and 7.

Table 2.16 presents a student schedule for either the two- or six-teacher team model. The student is in reading/language arts and mathematics modules

1 and 2. Each of these classes meets for 90 minutes each day of the year. In module 3, semester 1, the student has physical education for the first 45 minutes. After lunch, the student is in art for 45 minutes for the first 18 weeks of the school year and music for 45 minutes for the next 18 weeks. In module 4, for the first semester, the student is enrolled in social studies for 90 minutes daily; for the second semester, the student has science for 90 minutes daily. Also in the second semester, the exploratory program changes to 18 weeks of computers and 18 weeks of world languages in the 45 minutes after lunch.

Table 2.16   Middle School Student Schedule

	Semester 1		Semester 2
1	Reading/Language Arts	1	Reading/Language Arts
2	Mathematics	2	Mathematics
3	Physical Education Art/Music	3	Physical Education Computers/World Language
4	Social Studies	4	Science

Table 2.17   Semester 1/Semester 2: Benefits and Limitations

Benefits	Limitations
• High school students are responsible for as few as four courses per semester.	• Teachers need training to utilize appropriate teaching strategies.
• Because a high school student is enrolled in fewer courses per semester, the model provides an opportunity for positive rapport between student and teacher.	• Curriculum support is needed for extended periods.
• Some courses can meet every day for extended periods.	• Timing problems exist with Advanced Placement and end-of-the-year state and national exams.
• The extended time periods provide the opportunity for teachers to utilize appropriate instructional strategies.	• In creating middle school interdisciplinary teams, teachers must be certified for courses they teach.
• Secondary teachers tend to take more ownership for student success when they teach fewer students.	
• In middle school, opportunity is provided for 90 minutes daily in reading/language arts and mathematics.	
• A two-teacher middle school team focuses on student needs as well as content.	

INTERDISCIPLINARY–MAXIMUM FLEXIBILITY

In the early 1990s, educators felt that extended time periods might be the key to improving student performance. The belief was that if teachers had opportunities to teach in extended time periods and used appropriate pedagogy for this scheduling model, student performance would improve.

Marzano (2003) gives some indication of the types of pedagogy that improve student achievement in his discussion of the importance of "Opportunity to Learn" (OTL). He indicates three forms of curriculum: intended curriculum directed by the state, district, or school; implemented curriculum actually taught in the classroom; and attained curriculum learned by the student. In order to elevate the degree of student achievement, he advocates an improved connection between the implemented curriculum and the availability of time (p. 23). To accomplish this goal and to implement a viable and challenging curriculum based on the myriad of articulated standards, he encourages schools to identify the content essential for learning and to extend the available time for instruction. As evidence for his position, Marzano cites Herbert Walberg's 1997 study of achievement in schools, in which Walberg found that a positive relationship exists between increased instructional time and learning. His studies indicated that the extended time contributed to improved achievement in 97% of the 130 studies (p. 26).

Additionally, Jackson and Davis (2000) expand the conclusion stated in *Turning Points* that students benefit when teachers control time to lengthen or shorten class periods to meet instructional goals and student needs (see also Carnegie, 1989). In the interdisciplinary–maximum flexibility model, teams can adjust their schedules on a daily or weekly basis when they determine that the academic concerns are greater than the need to maintain fixed class periods. These decisions are discussed and determined during the common team plan time (Kasak, 2001; Merenbloom, 1991).

As demonstrated in the longitudinal study of middle-grade school reform conducted by Felner, Jackson, Kasak, Mulhall, Brand, and Flowers (1997), increased student achievement occurred in schools and teams that achieved a high level of implementation of the eight recommendations of *Turning Points*. Among those recommendations is the creation of smaller learning communities in which teams of teachers have control over time to meet the demands of a challenging, relevant curriculum (Carnegie, 1989).

Besides the studies that address middle school team issues, the NASSP (1996) study, *Breaking Ranks*, recommends the adoption of flexible time schedules in high schools. The report includes ideas about how a team of high school teachers could use flexible time modules to support their curriculum and their students' needs.

According to a survey of high school principals, the primary reason for adopting a block schedule format is to expand student course choices and eliminate study halls. However, the expanded use of time influenced the secondary reasons: to improve the quality of the student's educational experiences and to facilitate more innovative instructional strategies (Hackmann, 2002). In support of breaking from schedules with fixed times, *Breaking Ranks* cites the

Report of the National Education Commission on Time and Learning (1994): "Unyielding and relentless, the time available in a uniform six-hour day and a 180-day year is the unacknowledged design flaw in American education" (NASSP, 1996, p. 47). Consequently, time becomes a factor in the choice of structural options.

Definition: First in a series of team approaches to deliver curriculum and instruction, interdisciplinary–maximum flexibility features a group of teachers who teach the same students during the same periods of the day. These teachers also have a common planning period to implement the teaming process, including flexible or creative uses of time.

An analysis of the interdisciplinary–maximum flexibility option in Tables 2.18 and 2.19 includes the following definitions and examples:

Table 2.18   Essential Components of Interdisciplinary–Maximum Flexibility

Component	Definition
A group of teachers . . .	• Typically, this is a four-person group: one English, one social studies, one science, and one mathematics teacher. • In the fifth or sixth grades, the team could be two or three teachers. • In Grades 8 or 9, a teacher of technology, foreign language, art, or physical education could be the fifth teacher.
who teach the same students . . .	• It is essential that the number of classes or sections on a team should equal the number of teachers on the team. • In Grades 5, 6, or 7, twenty-five students may form a traveling section that will move together from period to period. • In Grades 7, 8, 9, or 10, a group of 125 students can be placed in a cohort group or small learning community. Students are then individually scheduled for classes with these teachers. A team control number ensures that students are only assigned to teachers of that team, house, magnet, or small learning community.
during the same periods of the day . . .	• All sections of the core subjects meet during the same periods. • Each team has its own assigned 5 or 6 periods for instruction. • Teachers' contracts determine the number of periods a team can meet.
and share common planning time.	• Teachers have a determined number of teaching or contact periods and a determined number of non-contact periods. • In many schools, one of the non-contact periods is labeled as a common planning period or team meeting. All teachers of the team are available at that time. • An agenda is prepared by the team leader to include student concerns, curriculum integration and delivery, and flexible or creative uses of time.

Utilization: To establish maximum flexibility, a common group of teachers must have a common group of students for the same periods of the day. In addition, these teachers must have a common planning period. Interdisciplinary–maximum flexibility is only possible when all of these factors are in place. In this environment, in addition to integrating the curriculum, teachers are able to implement the following:

Table 2.19   Examples of Flexibility

Concept	*Strategy*
Alter the sequence of classes.	• Students and teachers function differently at different times in the day. • Sequence could change from 1, 2, 3, 5, 6, 7 to 6, 7, 5, 1, 3, 2.
Plan large group instruction.	• A film, guest speaker, or teacher preparing the team for a field trip could address students in a large group setting. • Classes could meet in the library or multipurpose room.
Extend periods based upon situation or need.	• Utilization of 90-minute periods should be based on instructional decision of the teachers. • Day 1/day 2 schedule could be implemented on a permanent basis with teachers' approval.
Group and regroup students.	• On temporary or permanent basis, students could be grouped and regrouped for various instructional reasons. • The team could revise original class rosters. • Students having discipline problems could be separated by placement in different sections.
Schedule project time.	• Students could work on a long-term project for fixed times each day. • Independent study could become a feature of the schedule.
Create time for interdisciplinary units/ activities.	• Students could participate in interdisciplinary units or activities in addition to or in place of regular class activities. • A module could be created for advisory or character education programs.
Implement flex period.	• Teams could have a period per day at their discretion to plan advisory, remedial, and enrichment activities. • In the middle school, full band and chorus rehearsals could be scheduled during this time.

Decisions about each of the preceding elements require the collaboration of the small learning community. Consequently, the importance of common planning time comes into play. Calling common planning time a "daily professional development huddle," Jackson and Davis (2000) emphasize the need for the team to focus on coordinating the curriculum and improving teaching practices (p. 141). These activities cannot take place without the opportunity for collaboration. Further, studies indicate that in order for a high degree of implementation to take place, teams need to meet at least four times weekly for a minimum of 40 minutes each time (George & Alexander, 1993; Erb, 1992; Erb & Stevenson, 1999; Felner et al., 1997; Jackson & Davis, 2000; Kasak, 2001; Merenbloom, 1991).

The interdisciplinary–maximum flexibility model is a valuable tool in transitioning students from the elementary to the middle school. Two- and three-teacher team models reduce the number of teachers a student has while also reducing the number of students a teacher has. Table 2.20 presents an overall plan for a three-teacher interdisciplinary team; Tables 2.21 and 2.22 illustrate specific teacher and student schedules.

Table 2.20   Interdisciplinary–Maximum Flexibility: Middle School Three-Teacher Team Schedule

1			
2	Reading/Language Arts		
3	Team Meeting	Team Meeting	Team Meeting
4	Math-01	Science-03	Social Studies-02
5	Math-02	Science-01	Social Studies-03
6	Math-03	Science-02	Social Studies-01
7	Flex Period		
8	Personal Plan		

Table 2.20 requires teachers with dual certification or elementary licensure. They have the same 75 to 80 students during periods 1, 2, 4, 5, 6, and 7. A team meeting is scheduled during period three and personal plan during period 8. All three teachers collaboratively design and implement a reading/language arts program for periods 1 and 2. Students can be leveled, grouped, and regrouped accordingly. In periods 4, 5, and 6, one teacher teaches mathematics, one teacher teaches science, and one teacher teaches social studies.

Table 2.21   Interdisciplinary–Maximum Flexibility: Middle School Teacher Schedule

Period	Courses
1	Reading/Language Arts
2	Reading/Language Arts
3	Team Meeting
4	Mathematics-01
5	Mathematics-02
6	Mathematics-03
7	Flex Period
8	Plan

One of the three teachers follows the schedule illustrated in Table 2.21. The reading/language arts class meets periods 1 and 2. After the team meeting, the teacher sees three sections of mathematics. In period 7, this teacher is available for the flex period.

Table 2.22   Interdisciplinary–Maximum Flexibility: Middle School Student Schedule

Period	Courses
1	Reading/Language Arts
2	
3	Physical Education: Day 1, Band: Day 2
4	Social Studies
5	Mathematics
6	Science
7	Flex Period
8	Art/Computer/Technology/Life Skills (Quarter Rotation)

The sixth-grade student in Table 2.22 has reading/language arts periods 1 and 2. For period 3, the student leaves the team for physical education on day one and band on day two. The student then returns to the core area for social studies (period 4), mathematics (period 5), and science (period 6). In period 7, the student is with one of the three core teachers for enrichment, remediation, or advisory or is with the band teacher for a full band rehearsal. In period 8, the student returns to the encore area for art (first quarter), computers (second quarter), technology (third quarter), and life skills (fourth quarter).

Educators in many high schools have realized that the goals of the reform or school improvement process occur via small learning communities as well as 90-minute periods. The interdisciplinary–maximum flexibility model facilitates a strong transition from elementary to middle and middle to high school. High schools planning school-within-a-school, magnets, academies, ninth-grade houses, or small learning communities should consider interdisciplinary-maximum flexibility as a structural foundation as indicated in Table 2.23. By determining the length of the modules, high school teachers bring their subject matter specialization to a flexible setting that best addresses student needs (NASSP, 1996).

In a ninth-grade interdisciplinary–maximum flexibility small learning community, the core teachers are assigned four ninth-grade sections and one upper level course. One or more special education teachers provide in-class support as prescribed by students' IEPs. The classes are scheduled for consecutive

Table 2.23 Interdisciplinary–Maximum Flexibility: High School Team Schedule

	1	2	3	4	5	6	7
English	Plan	9-01 Above Average	9-02 Above Average	Team Meeting	9-01 Average	9-02 Average	Yearbook
Social Studies	Plan	9-02 Above Average	9-01 Above Average	Team Meeting	9-02 Average	9-01 Average	AP Government
Mathematics	Geometry	Math 9-01	Math 9-02	Team Meeting	Algebra I-01	Algebra I-02	Plan
Science	AP Biology	Science 9-02	Science 9-01	Team Meeting	Biology-02	Biology-01	Plan
Special Education		In-Class Support	In-Class Support	Team Meeting	In-Class Support	In-Class Support	

periods: 2, 3, 5, and 6. To allow teachers to arrange extended time periods as well as the other features of maximum flexibility, classes do not travel together for these four periods. Instead, pupils are individually scheduled using a team control number that ensures that these 100 students are with these four teachers periods 2, 3, 5, and 6. The next three Tables, 2.24, 2.25.and 2.26, illustrate teacher and student schedules for Grade 9 as well as a magnet technology model for Grades 10 and 11.

In Table 2.24, the schedule for a ninth-grade English teacher includes four periods of English 9. The teacher is also responsible for the school yearbook. Team meeting is period four; personal plan is period 1. On some days, the sequence of sections for periods 2, 3, 5, and 6 could change.

Table 2.24 Interdisciplinary–Maximum Flexibility: High School Teacher Schedule

1	Plan
2	English 9-01
3	English 9-02
4	Team Meeting
5	English 9-03
6	English 9-04
7	Yearbook-01

Table 2.25   Interdisciplinary–Maximum Flexibility: High School Student Schedule

1	Spanish II
2	English 9
3	Science 9
4	Band
5	Social Studies
6	Mathematics
7	Physical Education/Health

As illustrated in Table 2.25, students are scheduled on an individual basis by the computer. Periods 2, 3, 5, and 6 are within the domain of the small learning community. In periods 1, 4, and 7, the student experiences elective or required courses beyond the small learning community. On some days, teachers may change the sequence of subjects for periods 2, 3, 5, and 6.

Table 2.26   Interdisciplinary–Maximum Flexibility: High School Magnet

	1	2	3	4	5	6	7
English	10-01	10-02	TM	11-01	11-02	11-03	Plan
Social Studies	10-01	10-02	TM	11-01	11-02	11-03	Plan
Math	Geometry-01	Trigonometry/Analytics-01	TM	Algebra-01	Algebra-02	Geometry-02	Plan
Science	Physical Science-01	Physics-01	TM	Physics-02	Physical Science-02	Physical Science-03	Plan
Technology	I-01	II-01	TM	II-02	III-01	I-02	Plan

The interdisciplinary–maximum flexibility model can also be used for magnet, academy, or house programs in Grades 10–12. In Table 2.26, five teachers are designated to provide the technology magnet program for students in Grades 10 and 11. During the team meeting, teachers develop an integrated approach to deliver the total curriculum using technology as the major theme. Students are individually scheduled for their mathematics courses as well as their levels of technological proficiency. In periods 3 and 7, students are away from the magnet for electives.

Table 2.27   Interdisciplinary–Maximum Flexibility: Benefits and Limitations

Benefits	Limitations
• Although students have subject matter specialists for each content area, opportunities for coordination exist. • Teachers can provide special interdisciplinary units and activities to meet unique needs of pupils. • Content topics are easily correlated using a curriculum map. • A skills program is best implemented when integrated throughout all disciplines. • A discipline code for the entire team can be consistently established, communicated, and implemented. • When teachers' classrooms are contiguous, problems in the hallways are reduced. • Students may change classes at times decided by team members. • Members of the team can implement flexible scheduling in various ways. • Special education teachers and students can be included in the team structure. • State and national standards can be addressed as a team function.	• The team structure becomes a high priority in scheduling. In the high school, the importance is equal to the placement of courses with one or two sections referred to as singletons or doubletons in the schedule. • The number of teachers on a team must equal the number of sections a teacher is able to teach contractually. • Districts must commit resources for a meaningful number of team planning periods. • Staff development for the team process is essential. • Teachers must be certified for courses they are teaching.

INTERDISCIPLINARY–LIMITED FLEXIBILITY

Definition/Utilization: Although interdisciplinary–maximum flexibility exists as the ideal approach to team organization, this option is not always possible. Staffing issues, teachers' contracts, and unique programmatic situations may preclude the opportunity for teachers to have schedules that enable maximum flexibility. A student may take a core course away from the team, limiting or eliminating flexibility. In the high school, the design of ninth- and tenth-grade school-within-a-school prototypes frequently includes one or more core courses taught by a teacher not connected with the team per se.

In interdisciplinary–limited flexibility, four teachers of four different disciplines are responsible for the same five classes or 125 students during the same five periods of the day. Each period, one group, or approximately 25 students, leaves the team for an elective course or a different required course.

The four teachers of the team have the same teaching times, the same non-contact times, a common cohort of students, and common planning times. Consequently, they are able to implement some of the instructional personalization and team planning available in the interdisciplinary–maximum flexibility schedule: to respond to student needs, to collaborate on curriculum, and to share engaging teaching strategies. Opportunities for flexibility, however, are

Table 2.28   Opportunities for Flexibility

Strategies	Interdisciplinary–Maximum Flexibility	Interdisciplinary–Limited Flexibility
Alter sequence	Yes	Not possible: In each period, some students are in other classes
Large group instruction	Yes	Not possible: In each period, some students are in other classes
Extended periods	Yes	Not possible: In each period, some students are in other classes
Regrouping	Yes	Yes
Project time	Yes	Must be conducted in regular classes
Interdisciplinary engagements and units	Yes	Teacher's portion of interdisciplinary instruction must be in regular classroom; cannot have team activity at one time
Flex periods	Yes	Not possible: In each period some students are in other classes

limited. A summary of the similarities and differences of the two formats appears in Table 2.28.

The benefits of this model over a traditional non-teaming model allow it to be an alternative for both middle and high schools. For this model to function correctly, a team control number is needed to keep the students with the same cohort of teachers.

The analysis in Table 2.28 reveals the possibilities as well as the limitations of the interdisciplinary–limited flexibility model. This option can be utilized at the middle and high school levels.

In Table 2.29, four teachers (English, social studies, mathematics, science) comprise the team for approximately 125 students. Sections of their courses are scheduled periods 1, 2, 5, 6, and 7. Honors sections are scheduled for English, social studies, and science; mathematics students are placed in Algebra I and Algebra II.

During each of the designated periods, 80% of the students are in English, social studies, mathematics, and science while 20% are in an elective or another required course such as physical education/health or fine arts. In periods three and four, 100% of the students are in electives or other required courses.

The computer assigns students to a schedule based upon three factors: levels of English, social studies, mathematics, and science; elective(s); and other required courses as recorded in the students' request files. The computer is

Table 2.29   Interdisciplinary–Limited Flexibility: Ninth-Grade Team Schedule

	1	2	3	4	5	6	7
English	9-01	9-02	Team Meeting	Plan	9-03	9-04	Honors 9-01
Social Studies	9-01	9-02	Team Meeting	Plan	9-03	Honors 9-01	9-04
Mathematics	Algebra II-01	Algebra II-02	Team Meeting	Plan	Algebra I-01	Algebra I-02	Algebra I-03
Science	Biology-01	Honors Biology-01	Team Meeting	Plan	Biology-02	Biology-03	Biology-04
Electives	✓	✓	✓	✓	✓	✓	✓
Other Required Courses	✓	✓	✓	✓	✓	✓	✓

responsible to balance class size in this process, especially when electives are spread throughout the day. In building the schedule, an equal number of sections or seats must be available each period of the day. Tables 2.30 and 2.31 reflect teacher/student schedules at the middle school and high school levels.

Table 2.30   Interdisciplinary–Limited Flexibility: Teacher and Student Middle School Schedules

Middle School Teacher	
1	Team Meeting
2	English 7-01
3	English 7-02
4	English 7-03
5	English 7-04
6	English 7-05
7	Planning

This teacher is assigned five classes of English plus a team meeting and personal plan meeting daily.

Middle School Student	
1	Physical Education/Health
2	English
3	Social Studies
4	Mathematics
5	Science
6	French
7	Art, Music, Technology, Family and Consumer Science

In periods 2, 3, 4 and 5, the student is assigned to the core team. French is an elective; physical education/health and the quarterly rotations are required courses.

Table 2.31 **Interdisciplinary–Limited Flexibility: Teacher and Student High School Schedules**

High School Teacher	
1	Team Meeting
2	English 9-01
3	Honors English 9-01
4	English 9-02
5	English 9-03
6	English 9-04
7	Planning

High School Student	
1	French II
2	Honors Social Studies 9
3	Honors English 9
4	Honors Geometry
5	Biology
6	Physical Education/Health
7	Band

This teacher is assigned five classes of English plus a team meeting and personal plan meeting daily.

In periods 2, 3, 4, and 5, the student is assigned to the small learning community. French II and band are electives; physical education/health is required.

Table 2.32 **Interdisciplinary–Limited Flexibility: Benefits and Limitations**

Benefits	Limitations
• Team approach is possible even with limited flexibility. • Team meetings are held during the regular school day. • Teaming in high school is more likely to occur with this model. • Opportunities exist for teachers to respond to student needs. • Opportunities exist to integrate curriculum and share ideas regarding pedagogy. • Teachers are responsible for same cohort of students. • Students receive individual schedules. • Teachers can regroup students for various purposes.	• Teachers cannot alter the sequence of classes. • Large group instruction opportunities are limited. • Teachers cannot extend periods. • Teachers on the team need to coordinate engagements/program with non-team personnel. • Project time and interdisciplinary units and engagements take place in content area classes only. • Flex periods cannot be established.

INTERDISCIPLINARY: ENCORE OR EXPLORATORY PROGRAM

Definition: Primarily at the middle school level, opportunities for interdisciplinary approaches to instruction could be extended beyond the traditional core team of English, social studies, mathematics, science, and special education. In this model, art, music, physical education/health, technology, family and consumer science, and world language teachers are able to participate in an encore or exploratory program.

Utilization: As shown in Table 2.33, four encore or exploratory teachers could form a team. Four classes or 100 students could be assigned to one art, one music, one technology, and one family/consumer sciences teacher during the same periods of the day. As in the English, mathematics, science, social studies cohort, these teachers use the common planning time to adjust programs to meet student needs, integrate curriculum, arrange for large group sessions, teach interdisciplinary units, plan for extended periods, and regroup students as needed. High school teachers of required physical education, art, music, and technology courses could also use this arrangement.

Table 2.33   Interdisciplinary Team of Encore or Exploratory Teachers

	1	2	3	4	5	6	7	8
Art	6 A	6 B	Team Meeting	7 A	7 B	Plan	8 A	8 B
Music	6 A	6 B	Team Meeting	7 A	7 B	Plan	8 A	8 B
Technology	6 A	6 B	Team Meeting	7 A	7 B	Plan	8 A	8 B
Family and Consumer Science	6 A	6 B	Team Meeting	7 A	7 B	Plan	8 A	8 B

Table 2.34   Interdisciplinary Team-Encore or Exploratory Subjects: Benefits and Limitations

Benefits	*Limitations*
• Opportunity to function as interdisciplinary teams is extended to some or all encore and exploratory teachers. • Encore or exploratory teachers have a common planning period. • Programs can be adjusted to respond to unique needs of students. • These teachers can integrate curriculum, including thematic interdisciplinary units. • Teaching strategies can be shared. • Encore or exploratory teachers can be creative and flexible with use of time as they (a) alter sequence, (b) organize large groups, (c) extend periods, (d) group and regroup students, and (e) create project time.	• The creation of an interdisciplinary team for encore or exploratory teachers must be a high scheduling priority. • This model must be reflected in the program of studies.

Four teachers have volunteered to serve on an encore or exploratory team. The four courses are required at each grade level; students attend each course daily for nine weeks. Each hour a different interdisciplinary team reports for this exploratory program.

COMBINATION TEAM

Definition/Utilization: Combination subject teams are similar to but smaller than interdisciplinary–maximum flexibility teaching groups. When schools are unable to create four- or five-person teams, teachers may choose to participate in this model.

In the first example, Table 2.35, an English teacher and a social studies teacher at the middle school level are paired. They are able to create extended periods for sections 8-01, 8-02, 8-03, and 8-04. With the cooperation of the two teachers involved, double periods could be arranged for section 8-05. In the second example, Table 2.36, a mathematics teacher and a science teacher at the high school level are paired.

In all secondary grades, the student enrolls in both courses to enable the combination process. In the high school setting, teachers may have some paired and non-paired sections in their schedules. During the common planning time, those teaching on a combination team are able to integrate curriculum, share successful pedagogy, and have maximum control over time for the 90 minutes involved.

Table 2.35   Combination Middle School Team Teachers' Schedule

	1	2	3	4	5	6	7	8
English	8-01	8-02	TM	8-03	8-04	Lunch	8-05	Plan
Social Studies	8-02	8-01	TM	8-04	8-03	Lunch	Plan	8-05
Special Education	In-Class Support	In-Class Support	TM	Replacement English	Replacement Social Studies	Lunch	Resource	Resource

Table 2.36   Combination High School Team Teachers' Schedule

	1	2	3	4	5	6	7	8
Math	Algebra II-01	Algebra II-02	TM	Algebra II-03	Algebra II-04	Lunch	Probability and Statistics 01	Plan
Science	Chemistry 02	Chemistry 01	TM	Chemistry 04	Chemistry 03	Lunch	Plan	AP Chemistry 01

Table 2.37   Combination Team: Benefits and Limitations

Benefits	Limitations
• Two teachers have all the benefits of interdisciplinary–maximum flexibility. • Opportunities exist for teachers of required courses to utilize the combination model. • Teachers may integrate curriculum as appropriate. • Opportunities exist for large as well as small group instruction. • Students can be regrouped for various purposes. • Students could spend two periods in one subject for several consecutive days. • Participation in discussions on curriculum integration provides hands-on professional growth opportunities. • Special education teachers and students can be an integral part of the team structure. • In light of the subject matter specialization of special education teachers in Grades 9 to 12, this model is more likely to be selected.	• Scheduling the paired courses becomes a high scheduling priority. • Courses for graduation or magnet programs are likely to be included in a combination team.

SINGLE-SUBJECT OR DISCIPLINARY TEAM

Definition: With the focus on student achievement in specific content areas, schools are looking at single-subject or disciplinary teams in addition to or in place of interdisciplinary models. In this approach, two or more teachers of the same subject or course may be assigned a cohort of students during the same period or periods of the day.

Utilization: To improve student performance, participating teachers can group and regroup students throughout the school year based on learning styles, performance on pre- and post-tests, or other modalities of assessment. In Table 2.38, two Algebra II teachers work with the same 50 students in the same period each day. Pupils benefit from the comprehensive approach of teachers who may possess complementary talents.

Table 2.38   Single-Subject Team: High School Teachers' Schedule

Mathematics	1	2	3	4	5	6	7	8
Mr. Bolster	Algebra II-01	Algebra II-03	Team Meeting	Pre-Calculus-02	Lunch	Geometry-01	Geometry-03	Plan
Mrs. Geisz	Algebra II-02	Algebra II-04	Team Meeting	Honors Geometry-02	Lunch	Geometry-02	Geometry-04	Plan

In period 1 of Table 2.38, 50 students are assigned to Mr. Bolster and Mrs. Geisz. Students work with both teachers during the course of the year and are continually regrouped based upon readiness, comprehension, or mastery. In period 2, Mr. Bolster and Mrs. Geisz have a second Algebra II cohort and, in periods 6 and 7, two separate cohorts in geometry. The printed student schedule could reflect both teachers' names as the teacher for a given period.

Team meetings focus on the delivery of curriculum, effective strategies for various subsets of the student population, ideas for remediation as well as enrichment, curriculum revision and integration, and the relationship between curriculum and state and national standards and assessments.

Teams could also be established for physical education/health, art, reading, or world language. In physical education/health, classes could be organized based on skill levels as well as students' interests. In some cases, reading and/or mathematics could be scheduled for a single-subject team rather than as part of an interdisciplinary team.

Table 2.39   Single-Subject or Disciplinary Team: Benefits and Limitations

Benefits	*Limitations*
• Teachers plan instruction in one subject for a cohort of pupils who can be grouped and regrouped for varying purposes throughout the semester. • Pre-testing, learning styles, and multiple intelligences can determine groups. • Specific course adaptations and special programs address needs of pupils. • This model provides opportunities for curriculum development, implementation, and assessment. • Student may have more than one teacher for a particular course. • Experienced teachers help novice teachers. • Enrichment and remediation can be offered. • The team structure could include special education teachers.	• Multiple teachers are needed for the same course. • At the high school level, the offering of several sections of a course at the same time increases the potential for conflicts in the master schedule. • The number of preparations per teacher may increase. • Teachers must agree on the daily essential learning and assessment strategies.

ROTATIONAL

Definition/Utilization: Incorporating the positive elements of extended time periods needed for learning the curriculum, a rotational schedule extends periods beyond 40 to 45 minutes but not for 80 to 90 minutes. Although the schedule is based on 40-minute periods, classes can operate on a 60-minute basis as well. Over a three-day cycle, classes rotate so that each class meets twice for 60 minutes per meeting (see Table 2.40). During the time allocation for periods 1–3, students have two 60-minute classes; for periods 4–6,

Table 2.40 Prototype of Rotational Schedule

Periods (40 minutes)	Day 1 (60 minutes)	Day 2 (60 minutes)	Day 3 (60 minutes)
1	1	3	2
2	2	1	3
3			
4	4	6	5
5	5	4	6
6			
7	7	9	8
8	8	7	9
9			

students take another two 60-minute classes; finally, for periods 7–9, students take an additional two 60-minute classes. Lunch is a separate module of time. Teacher non-contacts should be spread over the day to enhance the likelihood of at least one non-contact period per day on the 60-minute schedule.

In Table 2.41, the teacher is responsible for four sections of geometry, one section of honors geometry, and one section of Algebra II. On day 1, the teacher sees sections 01, 02, and 03 of geometry as well as the honors geometry class plus a study hall. On day 2, the teacher sees sections 01, 03, and 04 of

Table 2.41 Rotational High School Teacher Schedule

		Day 1	Day 2	Day 3
1	Geometry-01	Geometry-01	Plan	Geometry-02
2	Geometry-02	Geometry-02	Geometry-01	Plan
3	Plan			
4	Geometry-03	Geometry-03	Geometry-04	Study Hall
5	Study Hall	Study Hall	Geometry-03	Geometry-04
6	Geometry-04			
7	Plan	Plan	Algebra II-01	Honors Geometry-01
8	Honors Geometry-01	Honors Geometry-01	Plan	Algebra II-01
9	Algebra II-01			

geometry and Algebra II-01. On day 3, the teacher has sections 02 and 04 of geometry as well as the honors geometry and Algebra II classes.

Table 2.42 illustrates a high school student's schedule. On day 1, the student attends English 9, Social Studies 9, band, Algebra II, technology or art, and Spanish II. On day 2, the student attends Freshman Seminar, English 9, biology, band, physical education/health, and technology or art. On day 3, the student schedule consists of social studies, Freshman Seminar, Algebra II, biology, Spanish II, and physical education/health.

Table 2.42   Rotational High School Student Schedule

		Day 1	Day 2	Day 3
1	English 9	English 9	Freshman Seminar	Social Studies 9
2	Social Studies 9	Social Studies 9	English 9	Freshman Seminar
3	Freshman Seminar			
4	Band	Band	Biology	Algebra II
5	Algebra II	Algebra II	Band	Biology
6	Biology			
7	Technology (Semester 1) Art (Semester 2)	Technology/Art Spanish II	Physical Education/Health Technology/Art	Spanish II Physical Education/Health
8	Spanish II			
9	Physical Education/Health			

Table 2.43   Rotational: Benefits and Limitations

Benefits	Limitations
• Rather than teaching 80- to 90-minute classes, teachers have the opportunity for 40- as well as 60-minute modules. • Teacher comfort with 60-minute periods could set the stage to accept 80- to 90-minute classes. • All teachers have the opportunity to teach extended periods. • Students benefit from the opportunity to prepare for six classes per day rather than nine. • Although the entire school is on the same schedule, interdisciplinary–maximum flexibility teams could explore benefits of operating independently.	• In practice, models of teaching/learning in 60-minute periods may not differ from 40-minute periods. • Teachers need to color-code the periods in their grade books to keep track of lessons to be taught. • Teachers may not be able to use the same test on the second day. • Careful orientation is needed to eliminate student confusion about the schedule for a specific day.

SUMMARY

As schools and districts review the reasons for restructuring or revising the master schedule, specific structural options or combinations of options begin to emerge. In refining the choices, options that aid the transition of students from elementary to middle school and middle to high school should be given strong consideration. As relationships emerge between the reasons for restructuring (see Table 2.44) and the options available, school and districts can begin to design programs to increase student achievement. These programs become the foundation of the master schedule to be developed.

At the outset of the process described in this chapter, school or district scheduling committees identified the reasons for restructuring. At this time, revisions to the list can be made, but the focus should now be on listing the structural options that complement the reasons. Rarely does a school choose just one of the eight structural options and proceed to build a master schedule. At this time, scheduling committees should create a list of options before proceeding with Chapters 3 (middle school scheduling) and 4 (high school scheduling).

Table 2.44   Reasons for Restructuring/Revising Master Schedule

		School	District
1.	Respond to student needs		
2.	Ease transition from elementary to middle school		
3.	Facilitate transition from middle to high school		
4.	Make effective use of available FTE positions		
5.	Increase or decrease the number of periods in the day		
6.	Lengthen the instructional module		
7.	Address state and national standards		
8.	Improve student achievement		
9.	Provide remediation		
10.	Establish houses, small learning communities, magnets		
11.	Move locus of control from management to teacher		
12.	Incorporate looping		
13.	Provide opportunities for inclusion of special needs students		
14.	Group and regroup students for a variety of instructional purposes		
15.	Establish advisory programs		

A Guide for Collaborative Conversations

To set the stage for further consideration of the eight structural options as well as the relationship between the reasons for restructuring and the options, the following questions serve as a guide:

Leader Questions

1. What methods should be used to present the options to the faculty and community?

2. What examples or graphics can be created to illustrate these options in light of the curriculum for the school or district?

3. Which structural options best meet our reasons for restructuring?

4. In what ways will the teachers' contract impact the options chosen?

5. How will the ultimate decision be made?

Teacher Questions

1. From an instructional perspective, which of the reasons for restructuring will guide this process?

2. Which options appeal to teachers?

3. Which options work best for our students?

4. Which options allow the best delivery of curriculum?

5. Which options enable students to meet state and national standards?

6. What training will teachers require for the options under consideration?

7. What impact will the teachers' contract have on this process?

8. How should the final options be selected?

3

Steps in Building a Middle School Schedule

A s middle schools proceed to identify objectives for restructuring and the organizational option(s) to accomplish these goals, the staff begins to focus on a master schedule for classes, teachers, and students. These schedules need structure and opportunities for flexibility within that structure to enable teachers and/or teams of teachers to control time, the ultimate objective for a middle school schedule (George & Alexander, 1993; Jackson & Davis, 2000; McEwin, Dickinson, & Jenkins, 2003; National Middle School Association, 1995). As stated in Chapter 2, Marzano's citation of Walberg's study (1997) emphasizes the positive relationship between learning and increased instructional time (Marzano, 2003). Consequently, the ability to control time increases the likelihood of increased student achievement.

A specific plan is needed to design this schedule. This process involves the collaborative work of administrators, counselors, teachers, and members of the scheduling committee. Decisions regarding the schedule should be reviewed in light of projected enrollment, special programs, staffing allocations, teachers' contracts, physical facilities, and other factors unique to the school. Of greatest importance, however, is the realization that the schedule should be directly related to the reasons for restructuring chosen in Chapter 1, the structural options chosen in Chapter 2, and student achievement.

ORGANIZING A MIDDLE SCHOOL FOR TEACHING AND LEARNING

The focus of this chapter is a step-by-step process for the development of this plan.

Review Reasons for Restructuring

As detailed in Chapter 1, the first step in the process is to recall the specific reasons selected for reorganizing or restructuring.

_____ 1. Respond to student needs.

_____ 2. Ease transition from elementary school to middle school.

_____ 3. Facilitate transition from middle school to high school.

_____ 4. Make effective use of available full-time equivalent (FTE) positions.

_____ 5. Increase or decrease the number of periods in the day.

_____ 6. Lengthen the instructional module.

_____ 7. Address state and national standards.

_____ 8. Improve student achievement.

_____ 9. Provide remediation.

_____ 10. Establish teams, houses, small learning communities, magnets.

_____ 11. Move locus of control from management to teacher.

_____ 12. Incorporate looping.

_____ 13. Provide opportunities for inclusion of special needs students.

_____ 14. Group and regroup students for a variety of instructional purposes.

_____ 15. Establish advisory programs.

In this chapter, an activity is provided for the committee to learn the skills involved or to complete each significant step in the process. Working through each of the activities listed provides the committee with a deeper understanding of each step.

> **Activity**
>
> 1. Indicate the factor(s) relevant for the school or district.
> 2. Note any pattern or relationship among the reasons selected.
> 3. Provide a preliminary expectation, description, or statement regarding the ultimate product—the schedule—in light of the reason(s) selected.

Choose Structural Options

The next step involves the selection of options to be included in the design of the schedule as identified and defined in Chapter 2.

_____ Day 1/Day 2

_____ Semester 1/Semester 2

_____ Interdisciplinary–Maximum Flexibility

_____ Interdisciplinary–Limited Flexibility

_____ Interdisciplinary-Encore or Exploratory Program

_____ Combination Team

_____ Single-Subject Team

_____ Rotational

Activity

1. Indicate the option(s) chosen for the school or district.

2. Note any pattern or relationship among the structural options selected.

3. Identify a pattern or relationship among the structural options selected and the reasons for reorganizing.

4. List the initial expectations for schedule design in light of the structural options(s) selected.

Create Bell and Lunch Schedule

Taking into consideration the structural option(s) selected, the faculty needs to see the outline of the bell/lunch schedule in concrete form. Two examples follow. In Table 3.1, an eight-period day plus a module (25 to 30 minutes) for lunch is the foundation for all structural options except for day 1/day 2 and Semester 1/Semester 2. This schedule provides three distinct lunch periods.

Table 3.1   Lunch Schedule: Modular

		1	8:00–8:45				
		2	8:50–9:35				
		3	9:40–10:25				
A		**B**		**C**			
Lunch	10:25–10:55	4	10:30–11:15	4	10:30–11:15		
4	11:00–11:45	Lunch	11:15–11:45	5	11:20–12:05		
5	11:50–12:35	5	11:50–12:35	Lunch	12:05–12:35		
		6	12:40–1:25				
		7	1:30–2:15				
		8	2:20–3:05				

Tables 3.2 and 3.3 illustrate a day 1/day 2 or semester 1/semester 2 schedule. Schools choosing day 1/day 2 use the example in Table 3.1 for eight-period days and Tables 3.2 and 3.3 for the days with extended times.

Table 3.2   Bell Schedule: Extended Time Periods

Periods	Specific Times	Number of Minutes
1 and 5	8:00–9:35	95 minutes
2 and 6	9:40–11:15	95 minutes
3 and 7	11:20–1:25 (includes lunch)	125 minutes
4 and 8	1:30–3:05	95 minutes

Table 3.3   Lunch Schedule: Extended Time Periods

Periods 3 and 7	A Module		
	Lunch	11:20–11:50	30 minutes
	Class	11:50–1:25	95 minutes
Periods 3 and 7	B Module		
	Class	11:20–12:00	40 minutes
	Lunch	12:00–12:30	30 minutes
	Class	12:30–1:25	55 minutes
Periods 3 and 7	C Module		
	Class	11:20–12:55	95 minutes
	Lunch	12:55–1:25	30 minutes

These examples can be modified to the needs of a given situation and help teachers to conceptualize the new schedule.

> **Activity**
>
> 1. Use the structural option(s) selected to create the bell and lunch schedule(s) for your school.
> 2. Invite feedback from staff and students.

Formulate Program of Studies

Simply defined, the program of studies lists the courses a student takes each quarter, semester, or year. Without a program of studies, a schedule cannot be constructed. Two major segments comprise the middle school program of studies: core and encore or exploratory. Typically, core includes English, social studies, mathematics, and science; encore or exploratory includes art, music, physical education, technology, health, and family and consumer sciences.

Due to the integral relationship between the schedule and the program of studies, important considerations arise:

- A day 1/day 2 schedule generally features eight periods plus a module for lunch.
- The day 1/day 2 and semester 1/semester 2 models can have two encore periods of 45 minutes per day or one encore period of 90 minutes per day.
- In order to move from a seven-period day (including or plus lunch) to an eight-period day plus lunch within the existing staffing allocation, core teachers may be assigned a flex period as part of the core block. When this occurs, core teachers are with students for six of the eight periods. In this case, additional encore or exploratory teachers may not be needed.
- Some states require a total number of periods or credits in encore or exploratory courses over the three-year middle school experience. These requirements influence the creation of the program of studies in each of the three grades.
- Study halls should be reduced, if not eliminated, in the middle grades.
- To increase the likelihood of implementing interdisciplinary–maximum flexibility, band and chorus should be grade-level programs. Multigrade band and chorus programs may increase the likelihood of interdisciplinary-limited flexibility.
- A nine-period day plus lunch enhances the possibility of multigrade band and chorus and the interdisciplinary–maximum flexibility model. With sufficient staff, teams from several grade levels could be in encore at the same time.
- Schools with interdisciplinary–limited flexibility that want to change to interdisciplinary–maximum flexibility need to add another required course to the core block.
- Remedial reading and remedial mathematics students might not receive the full encore or exploratory program.

The examples in Tables 3.4, 3.5, and 3.6 represent possible approaches to the necessary considerations for developing the program of studies.

Activity

1. Identify the factors that will guide the creation of the program of studies.

2. Create two or three program-of-studies options for the faculty and community to consider. Obtain feedback from the faculty and community on each option.

3. Describe how each option in the program of studies aligns with the reasons for restructuring, structural options, and state/national standards.

Projected Enrollment

The projected enrollment for the next school year impacts the number of teaching sections possible in the master schedule. Additionally, in calculating

Table 3.4 Program of Studies for Interdisciplinary–Maximum Flexibility: Eight-Period Day

Grade 6		Grade 7		Grade 8	
Core		**Core**		**Core**	
Reading/Language Arts	10.0	Reading/Language Arts	10.0	Reading/Language Arts	10.0
Social Studies	5.0	Social Studies	5.0	Social Studies	5.0
Math	5.0	Math	5.0	Math	5.0
Science	5.0	Science	5.0	Science	5.0
Total Core	25.0	Total Core	25.0	Total Core	25.0
Encore		**Encore**		**Encore**	
Day 1: Physical Education Day 2: Band, Chorus, Orchestra, or General Music	5.0	Day 1: Physical Education Day 2: Band, Chorus, Orchestra, or General Music	5.0	Day 1: Physical Education Day 2: Band, Chorus, Orchestra, or General Music	5.0
Trimesters: Art, Technology, Family and Consumer Science	5.0	Choose 1: French, Spanish, German, or Remedial Reading/Math	5.0	Choose 1: French, Spanish, German, or Remedial Reading/Math	5.0
Health	5.0	Quarters: Art, Technology, Family and Consumer Science, Health	5.0	Quarters: Art, Technology, Family and Consumer Science, Health	5.0
Total Encore	15.0	Total Encore	15.0	Total Encore	15.0
Total Periods	**40.0**	**Total Periods**	**40.0**	**Total Periods**	**40.0**

sections, core classes require sufficient seating for special needs and bilingual students to be included. Hines (2001) reports that the National Education Association recommends an inclusive class size of 28 of which no more than 25% are special needs students. Since special needs students might be in more required encore or exploratory classes than core classes, the number of encore or exploratory sections might be greater than the number of core sections. Consequently, careful consideration of the allocation of teaching sections is needed. By completing the chart in Table 3.7, the scheduling committee can best calculate the number of sections needed in each grade level.

> **Activity**
>
> 1. Complete the projected enrollment chart in Table 3.7 for the coming school year.
> 2. Determine the number of core sections needed, including seats for special needs students.
> 3. Estimate average class size for core sections.
> 4. Calculate the number of encore or exploratory sections needed for all students.
> 5. Project average class size for encore or exploratory classes.

Table 3.5 Program of Studies for Interdisciplinary–Maximum Flexibility: Day 1/Day 2, Sample A

Grade 6		Grade 7		Grade 8	
Core		**Core**		**Core**	
Reading/Language Arts	10.0	Reading/Language Arts	10.0	Reading/Language Arts	10.0
Social Studies	5.0	Social Studies	5.0	Social Studies	5.0
Mathematics	10.0	Mathematics	10.0	Mathematics	10.0
Science	5.0	Science	5.0	Science	5.0
Total Core	30.0	Total Core	30.0	Total Core	30.0
Encore		**Encore**		**Encore**	
Day 1: Physical Education	5.0	Day 1: Physical Education	5.0	Day 1: Physical Education	5.0
Day 2: Band, Chorus, or General Music		Day 2: Band, Chorus, or General Music		Day 2: Band, Chorus, or General Music	5.0
Choose 4: Art, Technology, Family and Consumer Science, World Language, Computers, Health	5.0	Choose 4: Art, Technology, Family and Consumer Science, World Language, Computers, Health	5.0	Choose 4: Art, Technology, Family and Consumer Science, World Language, Computers, Health	5.0
Total Encore	10.0	Total Encore	10.0	Total Encore	10.0
Total Periods	**40.0**	**Total Periods**	**40.0**	**Total Periods**	**40.0**

Decide Team Composition

As an outcome of the projected enrollment process, teams are formed. Based on the number of core sections at a grade level, teams can have 2, 3, 4, 5, or 6 sections. Special education teachers should be assigned to teams. Teams can consist of students from more than one grade level.

Table 3.8 presents possible options for teams along with teacher assignments.

> **Activity**
>
> Complete the chart in Table 3.9. Begin by entering the number of core sections (including special education) per grade level. Distribute that number among the desired options. For example, a school may have nine sections of core in Grade 6. One option would be to have three teams of three teachers plus special education on each team.

Table 3.6 Program of Studies for Interdisciplinary-Maximum Flexibility: Day 1/Day 2, Sample B

Grade 6		Grade 7		Grade 8	
Core		**Core**		**Core**	
Reading/Language Arts	10.0	Reading/Language Arts	10.0	Reading/Language Arts	10.0
Social Studies	5.0	Social Studies	5.0	Social Studies	5.0
Mathematics	5.0	Mathematics	5.0	Mathematics	5.0
Science	5.0	Science	5.0	Science	5.0
Flex	5.0	World Language	5.0	World Language	5.0
Total Core	30.0	Total Core	30.0	Total Core	30.0
Encore		**Encore**		**Encore**	
Day 1: Physical Education Day 2: Band, Chorus, or General Music	5.0	Day 1: Physical Education Day 2: Band, Chorus, or General Music	5.0	Day 1: Physical Education Day 2: Band, Chorus, or General Music	5.0
Choose 4: Art, Technology, Family and Consumer Science, World Language, Computers, Health	5.0	Choose 2: Art, Technology, Family and Consumer Science, Health	5.0	Choose 2: Art, Technology, Family and Consumer Science, Health	5.0
Total Encore	10.0	Total Encore	10.0	Total Encore	10.0
Total Periods	**40.0**	**Total Periods**	**40.0**	**Total Periods**	**40.0**

Table 3.7 Projected Enrollment Worksheet

	Grade 6	Grade 7	Grade 8
Regular Education			
Special Education-inclusion			
Special Education-self-contained			
ESL			
Other:			
Other:			
Total number of students			
Number of Core Sections			
Number of Encore Sections			

Table 3.8   Teaming Options

Two core teachers plus a special education teacher:
 	
    Language Arts/Social Studies/Reading
    Mathematics/Science/Reading
    Special Education
	Three core teachers plus a special education teacher:
	
	    Language Arts/Reading + Social Studies
	    Language Arts/Reading + Mathematics
	    Language Arts/Reading + Science
	    Special Education

Four core teachers plus a special education teacher:
 	
    Language Arts + Reading
    Social Studies + Reading
    Mathematics + Reading
    Science + Reading
    Special Education
	Four core teachers plus a special education teacher:
	
	    Language Arts + Flex/Advisory
	    Social Studies + Flex/Advisory
	    Mathematics + Flex/Advisory
	    Science + Flex/Advisory
	    Special Education

Five core teachers plus a special education teacher:
 	
    Language Arts
    Social Studies
    Mathematics
    Science
    World Language
    Special Education
	Six core teachers plus a special education teacher:
	    Language Arts/Reading 1
	    Mathematics 1
	    Social Studies
	    Science
	    Language Arts/Reading 2
	    Mathematics 2
	    Special Education

Table 3.9   Identification of Number of Core Teams per Grade Level Based Upon Enrollment

Grade	Number of Sections for Core	2 + Special Education	3 + Special Education	4 + Special Education	5 + Special Education	6 + Special Education
6						
7						
8						
Total						

Develop a Blueprint

As in an architectural plan, a blueprint guides the construction of a middle school schedule. Because a limited number of students can be in the cafeteria and encore or exploratory classrooms at a given time, the lunch and encore/exploratory periods need to be spread throughout the day.

Time is designated for core teachers to teach as well as to send classes to encore or exploratory courses. While students are at encore or exploratory classes, core teachers participate in team meetings and planning periods. To enhance opportunities for extended periods and flexibility, core and encore or exploratory teachers should teach consecutive periods. The three sample blueprints in Tables 3.10, 3.11, and 3.12 illustrate this concept of consecutive periods in the blueprint.

Table 3.10   Blueprint for Interdisciplinary–Maximum Flexibility: Lunch as a Module

	Grade 6	Grade 7	Grade 8
1	Core	Encore	Core
2	Core	Core	Encore
3	Encore	Core	Core
4	Core	Encore	Core
		Lunch Module	
5	Core	Core	Encore
			Lunch Module
6	Core	Core	Encore
	Lunch Module		
7	Encore	Core	Core
8	Encore	Encore	Core

Table 3.11   Blueprint for Interdisciplinary–Maximum Flexibility: Lunch as Full Period

	Grade 6	Grade 7	Grade 8
1	Core	Core	Encore
2	Core	Core	Encore
3	Core	Core	Core
4	Encore	Lunch	Core
5	Lunch	Core	Core
6	Encore	Core	Lunch
7	Core	Encore	Core
8	Core	Encore	Core

Table 3.12 Blueprint for Interdisciplinary–Maximum Flexibility, Day 1/Day 2: Lunch as a Module

	Grade 6	Grade 7	Grade 8
1	Core	Core	Core
2	Core	Core	Encore
3	Core	Encore	Core
4	Encore	Core	Core
5	Core	Core	Core
6	Core	Core	Encore
7	Core	Encore	Core
8	Encore	Core	Core

In day 1/day 2 schedules, at least one encore or exploratory period is needed in periods 1–4 and at least one in periods 5–8.

Activity

1. Determine the number of core and encore periods in the school day by using information from the program of studies.

2. Place the core and encore or exploratory periods on the blueprint by grade level.

3. Decide if lunch will be a period or a module.

4. Calculate the number of lunch modules or periods needed.

5. Confirm the student capacity of the encore or exploratory program for a given period.

6. Decide the number of classes, teams, or grade levels that can be in encore or exploratory at the same time.

7. Use the model in Table 3.13 to design a blueprint for your school.

Table 3.13 Blueprint Prototype

	Grade	Grade	Grade
1			
2			
3			
4			
5			
6			
7			
8			

Assemble the Grid of Teachers' Assignments

The grid is the actual schedule of teachers' assignments that emerges from the steps in building a schedule: reasons for reorganization, structural options, bell and lunch schedules, program of studies, projected enrollment, teaming decisions, and blueprint.

Three grid segments appear in Tables 3.14, 3.15, and 3.16. In Table 3.14, the students may be regrouped for ELA and then move into traveling sections for social studies, math, and science. In Table 3.15, the students are grouped heterogeneously and re-sorted each period. Leveling occurs only in mathematics.

Table 3.14   Grid of Teachers' Assignments: Grade 6 Core

	1	2	3	4	5	6	7	8
Team 6A								
Mr. Odom	ELA-01	ELA-01	Team Meeting	Lunch	SS-01	SS-02	SS-03	Plan
Mrs. Allesi	ELA-02	ELA-02	Team Meeting	Lunch	Math-03	Math-01	Math-02	Plan
Mr. Wilson	ELA-03	ELA-03	Team Meeting	Lunch	Science-02	Science-03	Science-01	Plan
Mr. Hassan Special Education	Replacement ELA		Team Meeting	Lunch	Replacement Math	Plan	In-Class Support	Resource

Table 3.15 Grid of Teachers' Assignments: Grade 7 Core

Team 7-1	1	2	3	4	5	6	7	8
Miss Brodnick	Reading-01	LA-01	LA-02	Team Meeting	Lunch	Plan	LA-03	LA-04
Miss Ferguson	Reading-02	Social Studies-01	Social Studies-02	Team Meeting	Lunch	Plan	Social Studies-03	Social Studies-04
Mr. Schlesinger	Reading-03	Science-01	Science-02	Team Meeting	Lunch	Plan	Science-3	Science-04
Mrs. Shenk	Reading-04	Math 7-01	Pre-Algebra-01	Team Meeting	Lunch	Plan	Math 7-02	Pre-Algebra-02
Mr. Gritz Special Education	Replacement Reading	In-Class Support	In-Class Support	Team Meeting	Lunch	Plan	In-Class Support	In-Class Support

In this encore and exploratory schedule, art, music, family and consumer sciences, and technology classes meet on an alternate-day basis. For example, an art teacher might have section 8-01 on day 1 and 8-02 on day 2. A student could have art on day 1 and music on day 2 for the first semester; a student could then have family and consumer science on day 1 and technology on day 2 for the second semester. Physical education classes meet daily.

Table 3.16 Grid of Teachers' Assignment: Encore or Exploratory

Encore	1	2	3	4	5	6	7	8
Art	8-01/8-02	8-05/8-06	Team Meeting/Plan	7-01/7-02	7-05/7-06	Lunch	6-01/6-02	6-05/6-06
Art	8-03/8-04	8-07/8-08	Team Meeting/Plan	7-03/7-04	7-07/7-08	Lunch	6-03/6-04	6-07/6-08
Music	8-01/8-02	8-05/8-06	Team Meeting/Plan	7-01/7-02	7-05/7-06	Lunch	6-01/6-02	6-05/6-06
Music	8-03/8-04	8-07/8-08	Team Meeting/Plan	7-03/7-04	7-07/7-08	Lunch	6-03/6-04	6-07/6-08
Family & Consumer Science	8-01/8-02	8-05/8-06	Team Meeting/Plan	7-01/7-02	7-05/7-06	Lunch	6-01/6-02	6-05/6-06
Family & Consumer Science	8-03/8-04	8-07/8-08	Team Meeting/Plan	7-03/7-04	7-07/7-08	Lunch	6-03/6-04	6-07/6-08
Technology	8-01/8-02	8-05/8-06	Team Meeting/Plan	7-01/7-02	7-05/7-06	Lunch	6-01/6-02	6-05/6-06
Technology	8-03/8-04	8-07/8-08	Team Meeting/Plan	7-03/7-04	7-07/7-08	Lunch	6-03/6-04	6-07/6-08
Physical Education	8-01	8-05	Team Meeting/Plan	7-01	7-05	Lunch	6-01	6-05
Physical Education	8-02	8-06	Team Meeting/Plan	7-02	7-06	Lunch	6-02	6-06
Physical Education	8-03	8-07	Team Meeting/Plan	7-03	7-07	Lunch	6-03	6-07
Physical Education	8-04	8-08	Team Meeting/Plan	7-04	7-08	Lunch	6-04	6-08

Plan the Staff Development Component

Once the schedule has been completed, teachers need an opportunity to work and think through the impact of the schedule on their teaching and the culture of the school. Zmuda et al. (2004) present Fullan's (2001) theory of an "implementation dip" that accompanies the change process when teachers fear their loss of competence. In order to recognize that emotion, the change facilitator needs to provide support and encourage adult involvement as keys to school-based change.

In the change process, teacher involvement remains essential in order to obtain teacher engagement and acceptance. Consequently, staff development sessions need to have a specific focus and not be a series of random and ill-connected workshops. To this end, (1997) caution that without a focused approach to staff development, the schedule change will be non-effective and may result in a regression to the previous structure or system-in-place as described by Dolan and discussed in Chapter 1.

To facilitate the staff development program, Chapters 5, 6, and 7 serve as resources to provide the necessary training for teachers to implement the small learning communities portion of the schedule. Chapter 8 is a major resource for models that support teaching in extended time periods.

SUMMARY

The dynamic process used to create a middle school schedule can be applied to schools with Grades 5 through 9. Individual situations may deviate from the sequential aspect of this process. In many cases, however, one step is the prerequisite for the next. In soliciting faculty acceptance and ownership of the changes, it may be helpful to look ahead to the concreteness of the blueprint and grid of teachers' assignments.

A Guide for Collaborative Conversations

To set the stage for further consideration of the steps in building a middle school schedule, the following questions serve as a guide:

Leader Questions

1. Who will participate in designing the schedule?

2. Who will ultimately be responsible for the finished product?

3. How can constituency groups monitor and provide feedback for the scheduling process?

4. How will the effectiveness of the schedule be evaluated?

Teacher Questions

1. How can the schedule be responsive to issues and concerns of teachers?

2. Who will be on the design committee to express the voice of teachers?

3. How can teachers monitor the progress of the schedule's development?

4. How can teachers compare the schedule being created with their initial expectation of the final product?

5. How will teachers learn to deliver and assess instruction in the new schedule?

4

Steps in Building
a High School
Schedule

As high schools proceed to identify objectives for restructuring and the organizational option(s) to accomplish these goals, the staff begins to focus on a master schedule for classes, teachers, and students. These schedules need structure and opportunities for flexibility within that structure to enable teachers and small learning communities to control time. Certain cardinal principles dictate the design of a 9 to 12 or 7 to 12 schedule. Once these principles are considered, however, the schedule can take a more creative bent. The fundamental aspects of a high school schedule follow:

- A listing of required and elective courses
- An opportunity for student selection
- A summary of courses requested
- A listing of singleton and doubleton courses (courses for which there will be only one or two sections)
- A conflict matrix to guide spreading singletons and doubletons in the creation of the master schedule
- Utilization of computers to create the master schedule, assign students to classes, analyze the loading process, and provide feedback on proposed changes to that schedule

Once these factors are identified, new and creative ways exist to design the schedule with the goal of improving student performance. The step-by-step process begins with identifying the reasons for restructuring in Chapter 1 and choosing the structural options appropriate for the school in Chapter 2. The computer software is a key factor in developing the schedule but does not displace the opportunity for creativity and for trying something new to meet the changing needs of students.

ORGANIZING A HIGH SCHOOL FOR TEACHING AND LEARNING

The focus of this chapter is a step-by-step process for the development of this plan.

Review Reasons for Restructuring

As detailed in Chapter 1, an initial step in the process recalls the specific reasons for reorganizing or restructuring high schools.

_____ 1. Respond to student needs.

_____ 2. Facilitate transition from middle school to high school.

_____ 3. Make effective use of available full-time equivalent (FTE) positions.

_____ 4. Increase or decrease the number of periods in the day.

_____ 5. Lengthen the instructional module.

_____ 6. Address state and national standards.

_____ 7. Improve student achievement.

_____ 8. Provide remediation.

_____ 9. Establish teams, houses, small learning communities, magnets.

_____ 10. Move locus of control from management to teacher.

_____ 11. Incorporate looping.

_____ 12. Provide opportunities for inclusion of special needs students.

_____ 13. Group and regroup students for a variety of instructional purposes.

_____ 14. Establish advisory programs.

In this chapter, an activity is provided for the committee to learn the skills involved or to complete each significant step in the process. Working through each of the activities listed provides the committee with a deeper understanding of each step.

Activity

1. Indicate the factor(s) relevant for the school or district.

2. Note any pattern or relationship among the reasons selected.

3. Provide a preliminary expectation, description, or statement regarding the ultimate product—the schedule—in light of the reason(s) selected.

Choose Structural Options

The next step involves the selection of options to be included in the design of the schedule as identified and defined in Chapter 2.

_____ Day 1/Day 2

_____ Semester 1/Semester 2

_____ Interdisciplinary–Maximum Flexibility

_____ Interdisciplinary–Limited Flexibility

_____ Interdisciplinary–Encore or Exploratory Program

_____ Combination Team

_____ Single-Subject Team

_____ Rotational

Activity

1. Indicate the options(s) chosen for the school or district.

2. Note any pattern or relationship among the structural options selected.

3. Identify a pattern or relationship among the structural options selected and the reasons for reorganizing.

4. List the initial expectations for the design of the schedule in light of structural options(s) selected.

Create Bell and Lunch Schedules

In light of the structural option(s) selected, the faculty needs to see the outline of the bell and lunch schedules. Three examples are provided. Table 4.1 illustrates a traditional nine-period day, including a full period for lunch. A student can be scheduled for lunch in periods 4, 5, 6, or 7. Schools with many singleton sections should consider maximizing the number of periods in the day to increase the likelihood of students receiving their first choices of courses. This bell and lunch schedule does not preclude small learning communities, magnets, academies, house plans, and opportunities for extended periods.

Table 4.2 illustrates a modular lunch schedule that serves all structural options except day 1/day 2 and semester 1/semester 2. In this example, an eight-period day plus a lunch module of 25 to 30 minutes, three opportunities for lunch exist. Additional lunch periods can be scheduled. It is more difficult to schedule singletons when lunch is a module rather than a full period.

Tables 4.3 and 4.4 apply to a day 1/day 2 or semester 1/semester 2 schedule. Schools that choose day 1/day 2 use Table 4.2 for eight-period days.

Subject to the modification necessary in a given situation, these examples help teachers conceptualize the new schedule.

Table 4.1   Lunch Schedule: Full Period

	1	8:00–8:40
	2	8:45–9:30
	3	9:35–10:10
Lunch	4	10:15–10:55
Lunch	5	11:00–11:40
Lunch	6	11:45–12:25
Lunch	7	12:30–1:10
	8	1:15–1:55
	9	2:00–2:40

Table 4.2   Lunch Schedule: Modular

		1	8:00–8:45		
		2	8:50–9:35		
		3	9:40–10:25		
A		**B**		**C**	
Lunch	10:25–10:55	4	10:30–11:15	4	10:30–11:15
4	11:00–11:45	Lunch	11:15–11:45	5	11:20–12:05
5	11:50–12:35	5	11:50–12:35	Lunch	12:05–12:35
		6	12:40–1:25		
		7	1:30–2:15		
		8	2:20–3:05		

Table 4.3   Bell Schedule: Day 1/Day 2 or Semester 1/Semester 2

Periods	Specific Times	Number of Minutes
1 and 5	8:00–9:35	95 minutes
2 and 6	9:40–11:15	95 minutes
3 and 7	11:20–1:25 (includes lunch)	125 minutes
4 and 8	1:30–3:05	95 minutes

Table 4.4   Lunch Schedule: Day 1/Day 2 or Semester 1/Semester 2

Periods 3 and 7	A Module		
	Lunch	11:20–11:50	30 minutes
	Class	11:50–1:25	95 minutes
Periods 3 and 7	B Module		
	Class	11:20–12:00	40 minutes
	Lunch	12:00–12:30	30 minutes
	Class	12:30–1:25	55 minutes
Periods 3 and 7	C Module		
	Class	11:20–12:55	95 minutes
	Lunch	12:55–1:25	30 minutes

Activity

1. Use the structural option(s) selected to create the bell and lunch schedule(s) for your school.

2. Invite feedback from staff and students.

Develop Student Registration Materials

Once the major decisions about reasons for restructuring, structural options, and bell and lunch schedules are complete, work must begin on the student registration materials and registration process. The registration manual reflects decisions regarding the organization of the school. Some of those decisions include the following:

- Ninth-grade small learning community or house
- Eight courses for day 1/day 2 or semester 1/semester 2 schedules
- Magnet programs
- Academies
- Work-study cooperative program
- Courses for combination team(s)
- Courses for single-subject team(s)

In the design of the manual, three key items require definition: graduation requirements, required courses, and elective courses. Questions to be considered in these key items appear in Table 4.5.

Table 4.5   Registration Manual

Key Item	Questions	Response(s)
Graduation requirements	• What courses do the state, school district, and/or local school mandate? • What courses are required for specific programs or diploma types? • What procedures are to be followed if a student fails one of the graduation requirements? • What impact will the new structure have on students' fulfillment of graduation requirements?	
Required courses	• Beyond the graduation requirements, what courses are required for specific programs, diploma types, or magnets? • Which of the requirements should be completed in Grades 9, 10, 11, and 12? • What opportunities exist for interdisciplinary instruction in light of graduation requirements and/or program requirements? • What impact will the new structure have on students' completion of required courses?	
Electives	• What electives are available for students in Grades 9, 10, 11, and 12? • Which electives are required for particular programs? • List any electives included in magnet programs.	

Once students have selected their courses from the registration manual and received approval where needed, course requests need to be listed, encoded, or bubbled-in on a scan sheet. By reviewing printouts of the data, administrators will know the number of students requesting a course, whether the course should be scheduled or cancelled, and the number of sections to be created. Table 4.6 demonstrates one student's requests.

Where needed, the course numbers reflect team control numbers, grade level, academic levels, and areas of concentration.

Establish Student Data Base

Generally, two files emerge as a result of scanning student requests: a course file and a student alphabetical listing. From the course file, administrators can identify the projected enrollment for each course. In some cases, a course or course level will be dropped for insufficient enrollment or combined with another level of the same course. In Table 4.7, a segment of the English file appears.

The student alphabetical listing in Table 4.8 is a data base that easily identifies the courses requested by individual students. As a result, a teacher, counselor, or administrator can easily confer with a student or parent to review next year's courses in light of achievement, program major, and goals to date. Additionally, students with incomplete course request sets can be identified.

Table 4.6 Student's Requests

Student Name: Julio Cortez	
Course	*Course Number*
English 9	1010
Social Studies 9	1020
Algebra I	1031
Biology	1042
French II	1051
Physical Education/Health	1060
Band	5306
Animation	1092

Table 4.7 Segment of English Department File

Course Number	*Course Title*	*Number of Requests*
1010	English 9	119
1012	College Prep English 9	85
1015	Honors English 9	46
1019	Inclusion English 9	21
9010	English 9 Self-Contained Special Education	16

Table 4.8 Student Alphabetical Course Request File

Name	Student Identification Number	*1*	*2*	*3*	*4*	*5*	*6*	*7*	*8*	*9*
Howard, Joshua	0798641	1010	2010	3010	4010	5010	7326	7816	8604	8605
Kazeer, Orlando	1384016	1011	2010	3111	4010	5111	5174	6151	—	—
Oskar, Hosea	2374161	1411	2407	3411	5611	5111	6203	6205	7118	7119

Administrators and department heads use the course file to identify students requesting courses that have prerequisites. The computer can print a list of all students requesting courses with prerequisites, such as Honors English 11, calculus, advanced placement biology, or French IV. This listing allows department heads to collaborate with colleagues for approval of those requests.

Create Department Summaries

Department summaries facilitate the organization of the school and effective use of teaching positions; therefore, a summary must be completed for each department. The mathematics department chart in Table 4.9 illustrates the detail of this managerial strategy.

A set of key terms is defined in the following paragraphs.

Enrollment numbers arise from the actual or projected number derived from the course file. The projected number includes any possible net change in preparation for the first day of the new school year.

Table 4.9   Mathematics Department Summary

Department: Mathematics	Enrollment	Sections	Average Class Size	Aggregate Periods
Algebra I	175	7	25.0	35
Honors Algebra I	100	4	25.0	20
Algebra II	257	10	25.7	50
Geometry	305	11	27.7	55
Honors Geometry	140	6	23.3	30
Trigonometry/Analytics	160	7	22.8	35
Probability and Statistics	85	3	28.3	15
Pre-Calculus	70	3	23.3	15
Calculus	64	3	21.3	15
Total	1,356	54		270

Sections are created for each course by dividing the enrollment into teaching groups. In many districts, a cap on class size exists for some or all courses. In general, however, the number of sections created is an arbitrary decision. In spite of the arbitrary nature of determining the number of sections, limits need to be observed: The number of sections cannot exceed the allocation of staff members for that department.

Average class size results from the course enrollment number divided by the number of teaching sections. Districts may stipulate minimum and maximum class sizes.

Aggregate periods reflect the total number of teaching periods per week dedicated to a course. For example, seven sections of Algebra I meet daily for the year; therefore, 35 aggregate periods per week are dedicated to Algebra I. If a full-time teacher could be assigned 25 periods, the school would need 1.4 teachers for Algebra I. Some schools may choose to offer the Algebra I course two periods per day or 10 aggregate periods per week. In these schools, staff needed for the seven sections of Algebra I (70 aggregate periods) would increase to 2.8. Aggregate periods directly relate to the structural option(s) chosen and the terms of the teachers' contract.

In computer and manual operations, a direct relationship also exists between the departmental summary and the assignments of teachers in that department. In the next step, categorizing teachers' assignments, every teaching section must be assigned to a teacher in a specific department. Based on a schedule in which teachers teach 25 periods per week, the aggregate periods total of 270 in Table 4.9 would suggest the need for ten full-time teachers and an eleventh person who might teach four classes. In another scenario in which teachers teach 30 periods per week, the same department summary would suggest the need for only nine full-time teachers.

Categorize Teacher Assignments

Each teacher's assignment is written individually, consistent with the structural option(s) chosen (see Table 4.10). In developing teachers' assignments, the numbers of sections, aggregate periods, and FTE positions assigned to a department are confirmed. The chart of teacher assignments is a major factor in creating the master schedule.

Table 4.10   Mathematics Teachers' Assignments

Teacher	Assignment	Aggregate Periods	Full-Time Equivalent
Ms. Carla Estrada	4 Algebra I [20] 1 Algebra II [5]	25	1.0
Mr. James Corwin	2 Algebra II [10] 2 Honors Algebra I [10] 1 Algebra II [5]	25	1.0
Mrs. Penelope Booth	4 Geometry [20] 1 Honors Geometry [5]	25	1.0

- Ms. Estrada and Mr. Corwin are mathematics teachers in an interdisciplinary–maximum flexibility or interdisciplinary–limited flexibility model for either a ninth-grade school-within-a-school or a beginning level of a magnet program.
- Mrs. Booth teaches a geometry-physics combination team for tenth- or eleventh-grade mathematics.

List Singletons, Doubletons, and Tripletons

From the department summaries, a list is created that enumerates singletons (courses for which only one section is offered), doubletons (courses for which two sections are offered), and tripletons (courses for which three sections are offered). The list provided in Table 4.11 identifies the courses needing further analysis prior to developing the schedule. The computer can assist with data needed for this analysis.

Table 4.11   List of Singletons, Doubletons, and Tripletons

Course	Enrollment	Sections
AP English 12	24	1
French V	19	1
Calculus II	17	1
AP U.S. Government	16	1
Pre-Calculus	31	2
Honors English 11	34	2
French IV	33	2
Honors Social Studies 11	38	2
Honors Geometry	65	3
French II	70	3
Spanish III	76	3

Generally, the actual scheduling begins with the spread of the singletons, doubletons, and tripletons over the number of periods in the school day. In some cases, programs such as ninth-grade school-within-a-school are of equal weight to the placement of singletons.

Formulate a Conflict Matrix for Singletons, Doubletons, and Tripletons

The software generates a conflict matrix, which provides information about the patterns of student requests. In deciding when to schedule a singleton, the scheduling committee needs to know what other courses these students are taking; which are singletons, doubletons, or tripletons; and when the other courses will be offered. Table 4.12 shows an example of a singleton: AP English 12. Using the data as shown in Table 4.12, the scheduling committee places the AP English 12 course in a specific period. The goal of this process is to increase the likelihood of students receiving first choice courses.

Although it is generally impossible to give all students their first choices, the person(s) building the schedule will attempt to satisfy all requests. The goal of this step is to create and utilize available data to spread the singletons, doubletons, and tripletons.

Place Singletons, Doubletons, and Tripletons on Master Schedule

Some schools or districts use software programs to place singletons, doubletons, and tripletons in the master schedule. Two prototypes illustrate the process of placing singletons, doubletons, and tripletons:

- Traditional nine periods including lunch (see Table 4.13)
- Conventional day 1/day 2 or semester 1/semester 2 (see Table 4.14)

Table 4.12 Matrix for Singleton Course: AP English 12 (Course #1089, Enrollment = 23)

Course Number	Course Name	Corresponding Enrollment	Number of Sections Available
1089	AP English 12	23	1
2095	AP U.S. Government/Economics	20	2
2090	U.S. Government/Economics	3	8
3195	Calculus	18	2
3193	Pre-Calculus	5	4
3185	Probability and Statistics	7	4
4195	AP Biology	12	1
4185	AP Chemistry	11	1
5192	French V	10	2
5142	Spanish V	13	2

Table 4.13 Traditional Nine-Period Schedule

	1	2	3	4	5	6	7	8	9
Mrs. Salazar	S 1015-01	S 1900-01							
Mr. Unitas				S 2105-01	S 2107-01				
Mr. Denkevitz			S 3107-01						S 3209-01
Mr. Donovan						S 4617-01			
Mr. Marchetti							S 5503-01		S 5919-01
Mr. Pricer		D 6363-01		D 6365-01			D 6365-02	D 6363-01	
Miss Mand	D 7979-01		D 7902-01			D 7902-02			D 7979-02
Dr. Owings		T 1217-01			T 1217-02			T 1217-03	
Mrs. Argent	T 2345-01				T 2345-02		T 2345-03		

A traditional nine-period day (see Table 4.13) maximizes the likelihood of students receiving first choices. A greater number of periods in the school day increases the likelihood of students receiving all choices. The illustrations below represent a segment of the master schedule following this key: S = singleton, D = doubleton, T = tripleton.

Conventional day 1/day 2 and semester 1/semester 2 schedules (see Table 4.14) involve eight instructional periods plus a module for lunch. This arrangement mathematically reduces the likelihood of all students receiving first-choice courses.

In a larger school, conflicts occur more often in Grades 11 and 12. These students are more likely to take courses that are singletons. In a smaller school, conflicts occur in all grades.

Table 4.14   Conventional Day 1/Day 2 or Semester 1/Semester 2 Schedule

	A1	A2	A3	A4		B1	B2	B3	B4
Mrs. Salazar	S 1015-01	S 1900-01							
Mr. Unitas				S 2105-01		S 2107-01			
Mr. Denkevitz		S 3107-01							S 3209-01
Mr. Donovan							S 4617-01		
Mr. Marchetti								S 5503-01	S 5919-01
Mr. Pricer		D 6363-01		D 6365-01			D 6365-02	D 6363-01	
Miss Mand	D 7979-01		D 7901-01			D 7902-02			D 7901-02
Dr. Owings		T 1217-01				T 1217-02		T 1217-03	
Mrs. Argent	T 2345-01		T 2345-02				T 2345-03		

Enter Remainder of Courses

Still using conflict matrix data generated by the computer, the schedule builder or scheduling committee spreads the remainder of the courses over the open periods in the teachers' schedules. This process is referred to as initial placement. In addition to monitoring the spread of singletons, doubletons, and tripletons, the schedule builder must also monitor the number of courses available by grade level each period so that each grade level has an adequate number of seats or courses each period of the day. Because students from various grades can enroll in the same courses, this monitoring is difficult. Table 4.15 is a managerial tool that can be used to achieve the distribution of courses by period and by grade level.

Table 4.16 extends the original traditional nine-period day schedule from singleton, doubleton, tripleton status to include the remainder of the courses. These courses appear in the schedule without an S, D, or T designation and

Table 4.15   Distribution of Courses by Grade Level and by Period

Period	Grade 9 Courses	Grade 10 Courses	Grade 11 Courses	Grade 12 Courses
1				
2				
3				
4				
5				
6				
7				
8				

Table 4.16   Traditional Nine-Period Schedule

	1	2	3	4	5	6	7	8	9
Mrs. Salazar	S 1015-01	S 1900-01		1013-04	Lunch		1013-05		1013-06
Mr. Unitas		2100-05		S 2105-01	S 2107-01	Lunch	2100-06	2100-07	
Mrs. Sabitino		3309-05	S 3107-01	Lunch		3309-06	3309-07		S 3209-01
Mr. Donovan	4100-08	4100-09			Lunch	S 4617-01		4811-06	4811-07
Mr. Marchetti	5716-05		5716-06	5716-07	Lunch		S 5503-01		S 5919-01
Mr. Pricer	6800-06	D 6363-01		D 6365-01		Lunch	D 6365-02	D 6363-02	
Miss Mand	D 7979-01		D 7902-01		Lunch	D 7902-02	7476-05		D 7979-02
Dr. Owings		T 1217-01		1219-09	T 1217-02	Lunch		T 1217-03	1219-10
Mrs. Argent	T 2345-01				T 2345-02	Lunch	T 2345-03	2346-04	2347-05

generally have a section number of 04 or higher. Later in the process, it may be necessary to move certain sections to other periods of the day to increase the percentage of students fully scheduled. Another reason to move a section is to improve the balance of the enrollments of each section of a course.

Table 4.17 extends the original day1/day 2 schedule from singleton, doubleton, tripleton status to include the remainder of the courses. Later in the process, as in Table 4.16, it may be necessary to move certain sections to other periods of the day to increase the percentage of students fully scheduled. Another reason to move a section is to improve the balance of the enrollments of each section of a course. This step represents the initial placement of courses in the master schedule.

Table 4.17   Conventional Day 1/Day 2 Schedule

	A1	A2	A3	A4	B1	B2	B3	B4
Mrs. Salazar	S 1015-01	S 1900-01		1013-04		1013-05	1013-06	
Mr. Unitas	2100-05	2100-06		S 2105-01	S 2107-01		2100-07	
Mrs. Sabitino		3309-05	S 3107-01			3309-06	3309-07	S 3209-01
Mr. Donovan		4100-08	4100-09	4811-06		S 4617-01	4811-07	
Mr. Marchetti		5716-05	5716-06	5716-07			S 5503-01	S 5919-01
Mr. Pricer	6800-08	D 6363-01		D 6365-01		D 6365-02	D 6363-02	
Miss Mand	D 7901-01		D 7902-01		D 7902-02		7476-08	D 7901-02
Dr. Owings		T 1217-01	1219-08		T 1217-02		T 1217-03	1219-10
Mrs. Argent	T 2345-01	T 2345-02				T 2345-03	2346-04	2347-05

Initial and Subsequent Runs

At this point, the computer merges two bodies of data—student requests and teacher assignments—to place students in available seats in the master schedule. Since the initial run may not place all students in available seats of requested courses, revisions to the original schedule will be needed. Revisions may include the relocation of a section of a course from one period to another, elimination of a section of a course that was not needed, or addition of a section of a course because of increased enrollment.

The key to identifying the necessary changes emerges from an analysis of incomplete student schedules and the sections not fully loaded. In some cases, changing the master schedule will increase the percentage of students fully scheduled. At some point, however, the decision will be made that the maximum number or percentage of pupils to be scheduled automatically has been achieved. When this occurs, the emphasis shifts from revising the master schedule to modifying students' requests. Identified students may be invited to reconsider courses requested in order to receive a full schedule.

Print Class Lists

When 100% of the student body has been fully scheduled, class lists can be printed and distributed to the faculty. At this point, the transition begins in the computer program from the scheduling mode to the grade reporting process.

Plan the Staff Development Component

Once the schedule has been completed, teachers need an opportunity to work and think through the impact of the schedule on their teaching and the culture of the school. Zmuda et al. (2004) present Fullan's (2001) theory of an "implementation dip" that accompanies the change process when teachers fear their loss of competence. In order to recognize that emotion, the change facilitator needs to provide support and encourage adult involvement as keys to school-based change.

In the change process, teacher involvement remains essential to obtaining teacher engagement and acceptance. Consequently, staff development sessions need to have a specific focus and not be a series of random and ill-connected workshops. To this end, Lipsitz et al. (1997) caution that without a focused approach to staff development, the schedule change will be non-effective and may result in a regression to the previous structure or system-in-place as described by Dolan (discussed in Chapter 1).

To facilitate the staff development program, Chapters 5, 6, and 7 serve as resources to provide the necessary training for teachers to implement the small learning communities portion of the schedule. Chapter 8 is a major resource for models that support teaching in extended time periods.

SUMMARY

This step-by-step guide enables the schedule builder or committee to create class assignments for students in Grades 9–12 or 6–12. Individual situations may require deviation from the sequential aspect of this guide. Although one step is generally the prerequisite for the next, in certain cases several steps can be completed concurrently or in a different sequence. The computer is an excellent resource for the scheduling aspect of school restructuring.

A Guide for Collaborative Conversations

To set the stage for further consideration of the steps in building a high school schedule, the following questions serve as a guide:

Leader Questions

1. Who will participate in designing the schedule?

2. Who will ultimately be responsible for the finished product?

3. How can constituency groups monitor and provide feedback for the scheduling process?

4. How will the effectiveness of the schedule be evaluated?

Teacher Questions

1. How can the schedule be responsive to issues and concerns of teachers?

2. Who will be on the design committee to express the voice of teachers?

3. How can teachers monitor the progress of the schedule's development?

4. How can teachers compare the schedule being created with their initial expectation of the final product?

5. How will teachers learn to deliver and assess instruction using the new schedule?

5

Small Learning Communities

Role and Function

Previous chapters focus on procedures for developing the master schedule at the middle and high school levels. It must be remembered, however, that the schedule is not an end in itself but a vehicle to promote teaching and learning. George and Alexander (1993) suggest that an effective schedule coincides with and serves the curriculum and programs chosen for the school or district. In order to achieve that goal, teachers require and deserve substantive, ongoing staff development that provides the support necessary to implement the schedule and deliver the curriculum. When the professional training is well planned and focused, opportunities for increased collegiality occur.

In an interview with NASSP authors (2004), former Executive Director of the National Staff Development Council, Dennis Sparks, emphasizes the importance of "high-quality teacher-to-teacher communication about teaching and learning" as a powerful professional development tool (p. 45). The ensuing adult relationships promote an atmosphere of trust in which teachers and administrators can productively dialogue about the effective utilization of the schedule. Restructuring enables two major phenomena to occur: small learning communities (SLCs) and teaching in extended time periods. The role and function of a small learning community is addressed in this chapter; a comprehensive goal-setting process to implement SLCs is introduced in Chapters 6 and 7; and structures that facilitate teaching in extended time periods are introduced in Chapter 8.

DEFINING SMALL
LEARNING COMMUNITIES

All small learning communities or teams have the same goal—to provide the best possible instructional program for a common group of students. Thomas S. Dickinson (2001, cited in Schurr & Lounsbury, 2001) suggests that the team's instructional goal is a mission to implement a vision that primarily focuses on student learning and secondarily on the adult benefits. Similar to teams in business, industry, or sports, cohort groups in schools must utilize cooperative and collaborative strategies on a day-to-day basis.

Senge and colleagues (2000) refer to teaming as "team learning" (p. 7), one of the five disciplines identified to promote organizational change. They maintain that team membership creates the opportunity for the collective dialogue necessary to achieve common goals. To this purpose, Arhar, Johnston, and Markle (1992a) cite the 1986 studies of Ashton and Webb in which teachers with teams report a greater sense of accomplishment as well as professional and emotional support. This opportunity within the schedule alone, however, does not guarantee the collaboration required to meet the needs of students. That goal must exist as a school priority and be actively supported by all involved. Moreover, the word and concept of *team* may have slightly different connotations for students, parents, and teachers.

Adolescents have a strong need to belong to something important and significant. This need was identified by the early contributors to middle level education and concurrently by psychologist Abraham Maslow (1968, as cited in Biehler, 1974). One element of Maslow's theory of growth emphasizes the need to belong, a need that must be satisfied before a person can move to a higher level of motivation. Consequently, decisions made by educators require keeping the concept of belonging in mind. The achievement associated with the student's experience of belonging also emerges from skilled teachers prepared to understand and meet student needs (Darling-Hammond, 1993).

Students may find it difficult to identify with a total school of 1,000 or more but can identify with a small community of 100 to 140 students (Merenbloom 1991; NASSP, 2006). For instance, being a member of a ninth-grade school-within-a-school can provide security and a meaningful experience during the transition from middle school to high school. The smaller cohort size creates an atmosphere of caring and investment in a student's academic progress by providing opportunities to develop teacher-student relationships and diminishing the fragmentation that often results from larger, more bureaucratic structures (Darling-Hammond, 1995).

For parents, the concept may be somewhat abstract since they may be unfamiliar with the terms as used when referring to school: team, small learning community, or school-within- a-school. On the other hand, parents can develop knowledge of and positive feelings about the team concept. Communication, student statements about what occurs in school, and opportunities to attend orientation sessions or special events sponsored by the SLC can provide concrete experiences (Merenbloom, 1991). Communication improves through teaming practices, keeping parents in the loop, informing them of their students' progress, and providing positive information about activities and assessments. In this way, parents form an integral part of the triumvirate of school, home, and student (Davies, 1992; Doda, 1992; Downes, 2001; NASSP, 2004).

The team needs to take measures to bring all parents into the mix. Communication efforts should include meeting the language needs of the diverse populations represented (Marzano, 2003). In the Steinberg, Brown, and Dornbusch studies on student achievement (1996, as cited in Davis, 2001), the level of parent involvement had a direct correlation with the amount of student engagement, success, and self-esteem. Parental involvement aids not only their child but the school's improvement process. One such parent views her involvement with the school as a watershed experience for herself, her children, and the children who will benefit from the results of her commitment. She shares her sense of fulfillment in *Educational Leadership:* "My work counts. My voice is heard. I've made a difference for my children" (Cavaretta, 1998). Her involvement reflects the beliefs of James Comer (as cited in Marzano, 2003), whose work proposes that parents form one of the three vital teams for school governments.

For teachers, the concept implies common planning, coteaching, and the integration of skills and content. George and Alexander (1993) refer to the interdisciplinary teaching unit as the "foundation of the entire middle school program" (p. 185). K. M. Brown (2001) cites the work of Capelluti and Stokes (1991) to emphasize the purpose of interdisciplinary teams: a structure that allows flexibility, creativity, and accountability; allowance of professional control over destiny; and enhanced productivity in working together rather than in isolation. Together, members of the teaching cohort make decisions that affect their students and the curriculum or that move beyond their classrooms. By implementing more collegial planning, students emerge with a better understanding of the course content in which they are enrolled (NASSP, 1996; NASSP, 2006).

The construct of teams, however, does not in itself guarantee the previously mentioned positive effects. Care must be taken by the members to build collegial relationships that will work toward meeting the needs of students, discussing and planning curriculum content and delivery, and using time effectively and flexibly. As teaching teams develop a comprehensive program for their students, their confidence grows within themselves and their colleagues. Ultimately, working in a small learning community provides a most enriching experience but one that demands commitment and evolves slowly. In this experience, three major components emerge:

- Response to student needs
- Curriculum integration and delivery
- Flexible and creative uses of time

THREE FEATURES OF A SMALL LEARNING COMMUNITY

Response to Student Needs

All students need a sense of being connected. Unfortunately, in spite of the educational reformers' voices heard periodically throughout the last century and continuing into this century, adolescent students have received short shrift, their physical, intellectual, social-emotional, and moral needs not considered as vital for their achievement. The results of this disconnection appear in studies by Klem and Connell (2004, as cited in Blum, 2005, p. 16) and chill the concerned educator: 40 to 60% of high school students have become "chronically disengaged from school." These researchers and others maintain that student connectedness is positively correlated with student achievement. Those students who do feel connected report a sense of belonging, a positive interaction with their teachers and other members of their school, school friendships, a recognition that their education matters, and involvement in extracurricular activities. Conversely, students who lack the same type of positive connections are more likely to indulge in at-risk behaviors (Blum, 2005; Capelluti & Brazee, 2003; Felner et al., 1997; Jackson & Davis, 2000; NASSP, 1996; Wheelock, 1998).

Respect emerges as a primary ingredient in developing a student's sense of connectedness. Alfie Kohn (2003) suggests that in our efforts to promote that connection the educational community continues to ask the wrong questions. Rather than asking how teachers can manage their classrooms so that students obey, we should be asking what do students need and how can we meet those needs? He refers to Sylwester's belief that misbehavior is a useful report that something in the classroom is not working and that the teacher needs to assess the real cause of the misbehavior; sometimes the cause may be events or relationships outside of the classroom and at other times may indicate that the content or delivery of curriculum lacks authenticity for the student. Tomlinson and Doubet (2005) present a case study in which the teacher, Katie Carson, connects with her students by honoring their prior knowledge. She engages her students with creativity and interaction but builds these characteristics into lessons that show respect for the understanding and knowledge they already possess. In this way, she makes the lessons and the learning authentic.

Small learning communities present educators with an increased opportunity to respond to the unique needs of students (Copland & Boatright, 2004; George & Alexander, 1993; Jackson & Davis, 2000; McEwin et al., 2003; NASSP, 1996, 2004). By focusing on physical, intellectual/cognitive, social-emotional, and moral development needs of students, teacher cohorts are able to develop appropriate responses to those needs and make special adjustments as necessary.

In each of the following sections, questions guide teaching teams in the development of a profile of their students. As questions are answered, student characteristics are listed in one column and creative implications and responses appear in the other. The charts become guides for team discussion, planning, and decision making. In order to be of maximum benefit, the process needs to be completed early in the school year and periodically revisited to identify changes.

Physical development refers to the muscular-skeletal growth and sexual development that occur at varying stages during the adolescent years. In completing Table 5.1, teams begin to develop a database by answering the questions below. Some responses will be entered into the characteristics column; others will be entered into the implications/response column.

Table 5.1   Physical Development

	Characteristics		Implications/Response
1		1	
2		2	
3		3	
4		4	

Physical Development Questions

- What levels of physical growth and development have we observed in individual students?
- To what extent are students aware of physical changes? What special activities can the team plan to address these changes?
- Which students matured early? Which students matured late?
- How can the team be responsive to individual differences and variations?
- To what extent do guidance or advisory functions address issues of physical development?
- To what extent do physical changes impact attention span, fatigue, restlessness, and/or need for movement?

Intellectual development refers to factors that impact individualized approaches to cognitive maturation. In completing Table 5.2, teams continue to develop a database by answering the questions below. Some responses will be entered into the characteristics column; other responses will be entered into the implications/response column.

Intellectual Development Questions

- What are the learning styles of our students? How can we develop learning engagements for each of these styles? How can we monitor the frequency of addressing each style?

Table 5.2   Intellectual Development

	Characteristics		Implications/Response
1		1	
2		2	
3		3	
4		4	

- What are the multiple intelligences of our students? In our content areas, what learning engagements address each of these intelligences?
- To what extent are students able to comprehend abstract concepts? What strategies best move students from the concrete to the abstract?
- What strategies can we utilize to enhance the concept development process? What adjustments can be made for students having difficulty with concept development?
- How do we utilize available student data to plan and assess instruction?
- How do we incorporate brain research findings into planning, delivering, and assessing instruction?
- How can we use the curriculum map to impact short- and long-term planning?

Social and emotional development reflects the degree of abilities for inter- and/or intrapersonal relationships. In completing Table 5.3, teams continue to enter characteristics and implications/responses in the appropriate columns.

Table 5.3   Social/Emotional Development

	Characteristics		Implications/Response
1		1	
2		2	
3		3	
4		4	

Social and Emotional Development Questions

- What are the major social-emotional needs of students on our team?
- To what extent is peer pressure a factor in classroom dynamics?
- What strategies can the small learning community utilize to reinforce peer approval and self-concept in constructive ways?
- How do we provide opportunities for all cohort students to know and work with each other?
- In planning lessons and learning engagements, how do we allow students opportunities for dependence, independence, and collaboration?
- How do we reinforce issues of social-emotional development in the context of our content areas?
- What strategies can the SLC utilize to handle discipline problems, conflicts between students, and/or particularly difficult situations?
- What discipline code is appropriate for our students? How can teachers consistently support the code?

Moral development describes the mores of the community in light of student maturation. Entering the information into Table 5.4 completes the database for the four dimensions of adolescent development.

Table 5.4 Moral Development

Characteristics		Implications/Response	
1		1	
2		2	
3		3	
4		4	

Moral Development Questions

- What are the major moral development needs of students on our team?
- How can teachers contribute to the implementation of the district's character education or values education program?
- How can teachers individually and as a small learning community teach and reinforce values such as courtesy, critical inquiry, freedom of thought and action, honesty, human worth and dignity, integrity, loyalty, order, patriotism, respect for others' rights, responsibility, self-respect, tolerance, and truth?
- During the course of the school year, how can the small learning community recognize those students who are leaders in values areas?

Curriculum Integration and Delivery

According to a position paper by Lipsitz et al (1997), developmental responsiveness forms one of the three characteristics of a high-achieving middle school. The other two elements, academic excellence and social equability, must be present to complete high-level educational experiences (Williamson & Johnston, 2004). Similarly, the authors of *Breaking Ranks* (NASSP, 1996) and *Breaking Ranks in the Middle* (NASSP, 2006) emphasize the connection between student engagement, varied instructional strategies, and an evaluation of learner needs. Those needs include real-world application of the curriculum. Wheelock (1998) encourages teachers to provide a real-world flavor to learning by integrating subject area standards and the 1991 SCANS standards defined by the Secretary of Labor's Commission on Achieving Necessary Skills. Those standards address workplace skills such as managing time and money, working in teams, interpreting and communicating information and complex ideas, and using technology.

Successful integration of curriculum arises from team or SLC discussions about the curriculum to be delivered. To begin, each member of a team or small learning community needs a firm understanding of what will be taught during the course of the school year across the content areas. Since teachers specialize in one or two content areas, each teacher is a vital part of the comprehensive interdisciplinary process. In order for team members to discuss their subject, they need to have available a variety of materials including input from district curriculum leaders and state and/or national standards. With this information, each individual teacher develops a list of the units of instruction for the academic year to share with colleagues. These lists not only guide the teacher but become the basis for the instructional program and, ultimately, the integration of the curriculum.

Pat Wolfe (2001) reminds teachers and learners to connect ideas to reinforce their impact on memory: "Learning is a process of building neural networks" (p. 135). Knowing this, teachers must consider that students learn best when they connect a topic in one subject to a topic previously or simultaneously learned in another subject. Further, students remember content or skills when they see patterns or relationships and can relate them to prior knowledge. Small learning communities or teams exist to make these learning connections. Numerous models of curriculum integration exist. Consequently, teams need to explore a menu of options and choose the one(s) that serve them best at their stage of maturation as a cohort group. Six possible options appear below:

1. Curriculum map

2. Interdisciplinary activities/units

3. Local, state, and national standards

4. Skill-of-the-week: basic skills

5. Skill-of-the-week: thinking skills

6. Reinforcement of advisory or guidance topics

A *curriculum map* guides the horizontal and vertical alignment of curriculum into a systemic plan. Teachers use it to make certain that the curriculum they deliver is the intended curriculum of the school, district, or state. In part, the map is a guardian of the curriculum, reminding teachers to continually prune their "stuff" and favorite projects that have ceased to be effective and do not fit the intent of the curriculum (Erickson, 2004).

Prior to beginning the actual mapping, team members complete some investigation of their content areas to help them initiate their plan. In addition to the essential content, other factors guide the entries: outside resources, learner levels, and teacher expertise. Since the mapping enterprise will become a dynamic part of the comprehensive curriculum, revisited and revised on an ongoing and as-needed basis, the format needs to be user friendly and efficient (Hayes-Jacobs, 2004).

Ideally, the team creates the map, using technology for revisions. Without a program or template, however, the process can be completed within the team meeting as a hands-on activity. To create an annual matrix of the subject units, each teacher uses a designated color of "sticky notes" to list the course units or topics by month. When all entries are completed, members of the team identify related concepts. Conceptual relationships form the basis for realigning the units or lessons so that similar topics or skills can be presented in several subjects at the same time, allowing for multidisciplinary integration without a formal interdisciplinary unit. During the realignment process, opportunities arise for the team to identify the organizing concepts being taught in the content areas.

Erickson (2001) stresses the importance of identifying and reinforcing the concepts: Without identifying the organizing concepts, curriculum documents

Table 5.5   Curriculum Map/Planning Matrix

	Sept.	Oct.	Nov.	Dec.	Jan.	Feb.	Mar.	Apr.	May	June
Language Arts										
Reading/Literature										
Social Studies										
Mathematics										
Science										
Foreign Language										
Art										
Music										
Physical Education										
Technology										
Family and Consumer Science										
Health										
Communications										

may address only skills. Educators cannot assume that students will be able to infer concepts or develop conceptual understanding from mastery of a skill (p. 47). From the identified concepts and instructional content, learning targets and essential questions can be developed so that students mesh skill development with conceptual understanding.

If actual alignment is not possible, additional opportunities should be sought to make connections such as discussing in team and announcing in class a strategy or concept to be taught in another subject at a future time. Through the creation of the curriculum matrix in Table 5.5, teachers help students see patterns and relationships. Those same findings contribute to the creation of interdisciplinary activities and/or units such as in magnet programs. However the map is developed, the proactive approach to integrating the curriculum benefits the entire team and creates a climate for delivering what Marzano (2003) calls the intended curriculum.

Interdisciplinary activities and units focus on the importance of making connections, of making meaning within one's own experiences (Wolfe, 2001). Studies indicate that teachers who have a strong content background and coordinate the integration of their curriculum with colleagues create an environment for high student achievement (Jackson & Davis, 2000; Trimble, 2003). Too often, students graduate from high school without an understanding of the connections that occur naturally between subject areas. This difficulty can be diminished if teachers ally themselves collaboratively beyond the department, forming groups that meet for the purpose of teaching skills in thinking or learning strategies (NASSP, 1996).

One logical source from which to choose a theme or topic for an interdisciplinary study emerges from an aligned curriculum map. In addition, a major theme or concept such as change can be selected. The study can involve two or more subjects that will create meaningful connections for students. Care needs to be taken, however, not to force a topic or theme. The unit must arise naturally from the aligned curriculum and may not be appropriate for all subject areas nor of value for the student. Further, teachers' forays into interdisciplinary instruction should be at their level of comfort and understanding.

Various forms of webbing present a method to begin the development of an interdisciplinary unit. The process used to create the web generates thinking that can be used within the classroom to enable student participation in the unit's development. The web in figure 5.1 is an adaptation of the organizer in Fogarty and Stoehr's (1995) work in curriculum integration.

The following steps facilitate the development of an interdisciplinary unit or major activity:

- Select a major theme or concept such as change, transition, man vs. nature, understanding self and others, exploration, decision making, loyalty, responsibility, systems, or patterns.
- Place a curriculum topic, such as the American Revolution or the American novel, into the chosen concept. Although not all content areas will be able to connect naturally with a topic, they will be able to address an enduring understanding or main thrust that arises from a broader organizing concept. If many subject areas are included in the unit, the concept must be broader and will be more abstract and more difficult to make meaningful (Erickson, 2001; Tomlinson, 1999; Wiggins & McTighe, 1998). Marzano (2003) recommends grouping essential learning according to its "sameness" (p. 118). The ultimate purpose should be to take student thinking to a transferable level in which students can recognize similar patterns in other areas.
- Construct a brief rationale for teacher use to conceptualize the unit and to serve as a basis for planning. The rationale should include:
  a. Selections from the curriculum map or listing of units for the year that have common elements, e.g., content or skills
  b. Organizing concept from which generalizations or principles will be developed as the unit is discussed
  c. Relevance of topic to student needs or theme of magnet or academy
  d. Standards addressed, unpacked, and embedded in the unit
  e. Enduring understandings or main thrusts for the interdisciplinary unit based upon what students should know, do, apply, understand, and/or explain

Each of the above steps opens the door for increased teacher discussion about the desired learning. Further, the discussion should highlight ways in which students can contribute to the design of the unit, perhaps by determining the enduring understanding or generalizations (Erickson, 2001; Tomlinson, 1999;

Figure 5.1   Interdisciplinary Unit Webbed Model

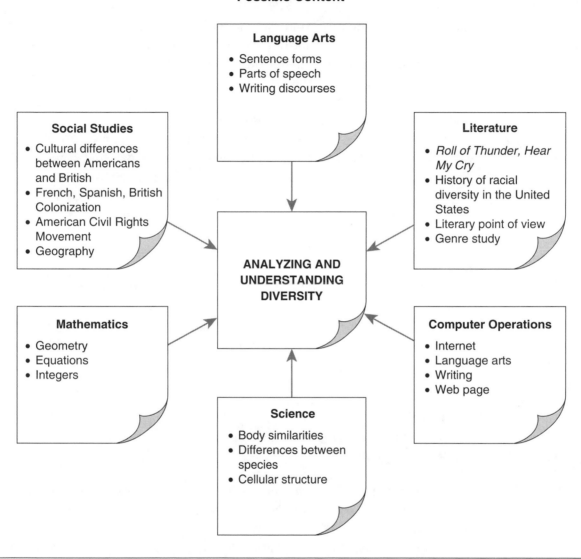

Team IDU: Diversity

Possible Content

Language Arts
- Sentence forms
- Parts of speech
- Writing discourses

Social Studies
- Cultural differences between Americans and British
- French, Spanish, British Colonization
- American Civil Rights Movement
- Geography

Literature
- *Roll of Thunder, Hear My Cry*
- History of racial diversity in the United States
- Literary point of view
- Genre study

ANALYZING AND UNDERSTANDING DIVERSITY

Mathematics
- Geometry
- Equations
- Integers

Computer Operations
- Internet
- Language arts
- Writing
- Web page

Science
- Body similarities
- Differences between species
- Cellular structure

Wiggins & McTighe, 1998). Comprehensive planning for interdisciplinary units is best accomplished when teachers work collaboratively to do the following:

■ Introduce the unit with engaging kickoff activities or an anticipatory set in large or small groups.
■ Develop specific learning engagements by subject area that answer essential questions, reflect state and national standards, reinforce specific knowledge needed, and aid students' success in both formative and summative assessments.
■ Maintain opportunities for formative assessment throughout the unit. Construct rubrics for consistent and equitable evaluation as needed.
■ Provide summative assessment to close the unit.

The inclusion of students in the planning process enables them to see patterns and relationships to an even greater depth.

Local, state, and national standards are worthy benchmarks that have the potential for unifying student learning. While most agree that consistency in educational experiences for all students is worthy, the manner in which the consistency appears is contested in the literature and practice. States do not have similar standards, state standards do not necessarily connect with national standards in specific disciplines, and teachers establish their own sets of standards for their individual classrooms (Wheelock, 1998). More important, taken at face value, the prevailing standards have the potential for fragmenting student learning rather than preparing students to develop concepts and employ critical thinking (Erickson, 2001).

In spite of these problems, however, teachers effectively use state and national standards to guide unit planning as well as day-to-day instruction. They recognize the need for suitable changes in instruction to provide students with the skills and content necessary to become problem solvers. Those educators truly concerned with the learning success of students acknowledge that too many previous practices prepared students for the challenge of trivial pursuit rather than concept development and the challenge of contemporary living. Practitioners hope that standards will provide the hallmarks and guidelines to enable them to make progress in meeting student needs and creating successful learners (Wheelock, 1998).

Although many standards apply to specific courses, some benchmarks or performance indicators within the standards apply to skills that cross subject areas:

- Use of charts and graphs
- Reading for main ideas
- Writing a topic sentence
- Communication skills
- Measurement

By including benchmark cross-curricular elements within the team's instructional plan, teachers embed the necessary elaborative rehearsal of a skill to place it in long-term memory (Wolfe, 2001).

As illustrated in Table 5.6, the small learning community or team selects a standard that cuts across several disciplines as the focus for a one- or two-week period. Preferably, the selected standard or benchmark appears on a more comprehensive curriculum map and can be correlated with the units to be taught in specific disciplines. This focus on standards should be ongoing and provide the basis for rubrics and assessment. The planning model enables each team member to focus on the standard.

Skill-of-the-week: basic skills represents an effort by teams to create an annual timetable to integrate learning skills in the context of each subject area. Some of those skills arise from content standards and standard benchmarks; others arise from direct observation of gaps in student skill levels. By identifying and reinforcing the chosen skill, the SLC sets the stage for students to develop automaticity, the effective level of procedural knowledge. The chosen time frame needs to take into consideration the degree and

Table 5.6 Integrating a Standard

	Brief description to be completed by team and individual subject teachers	
Standard		
Time Period Start		
Stop		
Introductory Activity		
Subject Area Content and Formative Assessment	**Content**	**Formative Assessment**
English		
Social Studies		
Mathematics		
Science		
Other		
Summative Assessment		

complexity of various practice engagements necessary to reach that stage of automaticity (Marzano, 2003). When the skill vision for the year has been completed, the teaching cohort begins to create an annual plan for the integration of each skill on a weekly plan sheet as indicated in Table 5.7 and discussed in Chapter 7. Possible skill-of-the-week topics include:

- Format for student work
- Finding the main idea
- Note taking
- Listening
- Outlining
- Identifying arguments to support a position
- Differentiating fact from opinion
- Verifying accuracy
- Cause-and-effect relationship
- Estimating

Skill-of-the-week: thinking skills supports the development of critical thinking for the student and, similar to skill-of-the-week: basic skills, guides teaching strategies for a defined period of time. Potential thinking skills topics include:

- Formulating questions
- Storing information
- Retrieving information
- Ordering

Table 5.7 Skill-of-the-Week: Basic Skill

	Brief description to be completed by team and individual subject teachers	
Basic Skill		
Time Period Start		
Stop		
Introductory Activity		
Subject Area Content and Formative Assessment	**Content**	**Formative Assessment**
English		
Social Studies		
Mathematics		
Science		
Other		
Summative Assessment		

Table 5.8 Skill-of-the-Week: Thinking Skill

	Brief description to be completed by team and individual subject teachers	
Thinking Skill		
Time Period Start		
Stop		
Introductory Activity		
Subject Area Content and Formative Assessment	**Content**	**Formative Assessment**
English		
Social Studies		
Mathematics		
Science		
Other		
Summative Assessment		

- Classifying
- Establishing criteria
- Identifying relationships and patterns
- Inferring
- Predicting
- Verifying

As illustrated in Table 5.8, the development of a matrix can be helpful.

Reinforcement of advisory or guidance topics supports the focus on adolescent issues in the curriculum and the opportunity for students to view these in the context of the day-to-day instructional engagements. The 1995 revision (NMSA, 1995) of the National Middle School Association's 1982 position paper, *This We Believe* (NMSA, 1982), reaffirms that each middle-level student should be connected with an adult "who supports the student's academic and personal development" (p. 16). This statement echoes the position taken in the original publication in the identification of the need for adult advocates for early teens. From its philosophical inception, the middle school concept included a guidance or advisory focus.

In 1989, the Carnegie Corporation's heralded publication *Turning Points: Preparing American Youth for the 21st Century* noted that an advisory system appeared to reduce student alienation and to encourage higher degrees of student engagement and learning (as cited in Burkhardt, 2001). In many middle schools, the schoolday schedule provides a time for pupils to discuss concerns such as understanding self and others, conflict resolution, communication skills, or decision making. The advisory program promotes an important result: ongoing communication in a community of learners and their adult advocates.

Today these programs occur in high schools, especially in the ninth grade. NASSP (1996) advocates the personalization of high schools to create an atmosphere of community in which students and teachers better know one another. Their report, *Breaking Ranks,* encourages high schools to connect an adult advocate with each student and help that student develop a personal learning plan. Further, they emphasize in concert with parents the importance of teaching the values upon which the nation builds its society. If the high school identifies a specific class period for advisory time, whole-group topics can be discussed: transition from middle school to high school, study skills, introduction to extracurricular programs, career development, and external testing.

Throughout Grades 5–12, topics often focus on character education. While the entire school may participate collectively under the principal's direction, teams or small learning communities can select a specific advisory or character education topic to reinforce in the context of subject or content areas. The advisory or character education content becomes more meaningful through this reinforcement, greatly increasing the likelihood of transfer.

Some ideas for topics follow and can be incorporated into the team's weekly or monthly planning as in Table 5.9:

- Caring
- Citizenship
- Courtesy
- Critical inquiry
- Equality
- Fairness
- Honesty
- Human worth and dignity
- Integrity

- Justice
- Loyalty
- Rational consent
- Reasoned argument
- Responsibility
- Respect
- Tolerance
- Trustworthiness
- Truth

Table 5.9   Reinforcement of Advisory/Guidance Topic

	Brief description to be completed by team and individual subject teachers	
Advisory or Guidance Topic		
Time Period Start		
Stop		
Introductory Activity		
Subject Area Content and Formative Assessment	**Content**	**Formative Assessment**
English		
Social Studies		
Mathematics		
Science		
Other		
Summative Assessment		

Instructional delivery includes teaching strategies or best practices appropriate to the curriculum and developmental needs of students. Following the identification of content and the choice of a method of curriculum integration, the next step for the SLC features a focus on pedagogy. Wolfe (2001) reminds educators of the importance of this phase: "The most powerful strategies increase retention, understanding, and students' abilities to apply the concepts they are learning" (p. 131).

Discussion of various strategies not only broadens the instructional repertoire for each teacher but provides a forum for meeting the needs of the students. The results of those discussions often positively impact those students who may have learning or behavior problems in one or more classes. Therefore, the movement away from nonproductive discussion about students into

Table 5.10   Sample Strategies for Consideration

Addressing Learning Characteristics	Brain Research	Cognitive Process	Literacy
• Use of hands-on activities • Cooperative learning • Address attention span limitations of the age group • Methods of providing structure for classroom activities, homework, and long-term projects • Differentiation of instruction • Learning styles • Learning stations • Student choice	• Chunking information • Visualization • Orchestration of meaning • Strategies for memory retrieval • Rehearsal • Anticipatory-set activities • Motivational activities allied with learning targets • Networking information	• Inductive methods of teaching • Concept development process • Transitions to connect aspects of the learning process • Simulations • Use of wait time • Integration of critical thinking skills • Structured learning experiences • Provision for multiple exposures to and complex interactions with content	• Teaching reading in the content areas • Reading strategies such as KWL, SQ3R, Freyer • Teaching writing in the content areas • Use of charts and graphs • Note taking skills • DED notes/T-notes

productive discussions about curriculum and pedagogy is essential for a high-functioning team (Hackmann et al., 2002).

When teams devote 50 to 60% of planning time to curriculum integration and delivery, a learning environment is created that will have a positive impact on student success and achievement. As in all other aspects of the structural change process, continuing staff development support must be provided to help teachers integrate curriculum, develop lessons, and utilize appropriate instructional models. In Table 5.10, sample strategies are divided into four major categories.

The significance of curriculum integration and delivery within the role and function of a team or small learning community emerges through daily and weekly discussions within the staff development process. Methods to be used in curriculum integration and delivery need to be incremental, adopting and adapting only those ideas that can be successfully implemented by the team and are relevant for the students.

Flexible/Creative Uses of Time

When teachers are able to make decisions regarding time, their sense of empowerment over curriculum and instruction heightens. They are able to fulfill the purpose of reform and restructuring: to increase student achievement (Hackmann et al., 2002). The additional time provided for students to make meaning of their instruction enhances their opportunities for increased achievement (Jackson & Davis, 2000; Marzano, 2003). Bransford et al. (2000) imply that time is a requisite for the construction of meaning so that curriculum is not rushed but thoughtfully designed to allow time for students to integrate complex ideas through engaging strategies and reflection. In the middle school, constructive use of flexible time also responds to the changing development of students, including physical growth changes and a short attention span (Merenbloom, 1991).

Introduced in Chapter 2, two structural options provide the best opportunity for flexibility: interdisciplinary–maximum flexibility and combination. These options set the stage for altering the sequence of classes, providing large group instruction, extending periods when desired, grouping and regrouping students, and scheduling project time or independent study. Ideally, the daily schedule should be a function of the instructional experiences planned by the cohort of teachers. The teachers adjust the time according to the discussed needs of the various subject areas in order to meet their learning targets for student achievement. As in the other elements of the role and function of the team, these discussions should be held while working within the structure of the weekly plan chart.

Teams using the interdisciplinary–maximum flexibility or combination models can utilize five strategies to achieve a flexible/creative schedule.

Altering the sequence of classes allows teachers to see classes at different times of the day. Students and adults experience variations in the levels of chemicals that naturally exist within their bodies. These chemicals influence the ability to attend to instruction. In the afternoon, the chemical responsible for drowsiness increases. Therefore, by alternating the sequence of classes, students are seen at different times of their attention cycle (Jensen, 1998a; Sylwester, 1995). This change provides both the novelty and the opportune alert time for improved attention.

In light of the information provided by those involved in brain research related to teaching and learning, teachers and students benefit when classes do not follow the same daily sequence. While advantages and disadvantages exist for seeing classes in a fixed sequence, teams need to discuss altering the sequence to maximize student attention. With advance planning, a teacher could experience each sequence of classes in Tables 5.11 and 5.12.

Large group instruction provides the opportunity for the entire team to meet at one time. The total number of minutes within the allotted time can be redistributed to allow for large group sessions. In this way, all members of the small learning community, students and teachers, can convene for a film, guest speaker, panel discussion, kickoff for an interdisciplinary unit, culminating activity for a skill-of-the-week experience, or readiness session for a team field trip. If either the interdisciplinary–maximum flexibility or combination option is in place, students do not miss any other classes while attending large group sessions.

Extended or reduced periods are examples of decisions made by the team of teachers in light of their instructional plans. In certain situations, the team of teachers can expand or contract the length of the learning module. As stated earlier in the introduction to flexible/creative uses of time, Jensen (1998b) reinforces the need for time by identifying three functions of time in the learning process: The various learning experiences need to be deliberate and not rushed, internal time or reflection is essential to create meaning, and learning needs time to gestate or set after the experience. The extended time allows the teacher to productively use "down-time," the time necessary for critical input to fix into memory. During this down-time, the type of instructional engagement changes.

Table 5.11   Altering Sequence of Classes: Interdisciplinary Team

	Sequence 1	Sequence 2	Sequence 3	Sequence 4	Sequence 5
Period 1	Section 01	Section 05	Section 04	Section 03	Section 02
Period 2	Section 02	Section 01	Section 05	Section 04	Section 03
Period 3	Section 03	Section 02	Section 01	Section 05	Section 04
Period 6	Section 04	Section 03	Section 02	Section 01	Section 05
Period 7	Section 05	Section 04	Section 03	Section 02	Section 01

Table 5.12   Altering Sequence of Classes: Combination Team

	Sequence 1		Sequence 2	
	English Teacher	Social Studies Teacher	English Teacher	Social Studies Teacher
Period 3	Section 01	Section 02	Section 02	Section 01
Period 4	Section 02	Section 01	Section 01	Section 02

In interdisciplinary–maximum flexibility schedules constructed with 40 to 50 minute periods, teams can create 80 to 90 minute periods when one of the teachers so requests (see Table 5.13). For instance, a science teacher may want an extended lab period; a mathematics teacher a longer opportunity for use of manipulatives; or the English teacher a writers' workshop. On a five-teacher, five-section, five-person team, one section will not have the opportunity for extended periods each time the sequence is implemented.

In a schedule originally created for 90-minute classes on a day 1/day 2 basis, the team has the option to hold 40 to 45 minute classes when desired. This decision does not impact any other team or group of teachers, including encore classes.

Grouping and regrouping students allows students to be placed in any of the teaching sections of that team for a variety of purposes. Although fixed

Table 5.13   Providing Extended Time Periods

Traditional	Day 1	Day 2
Period 1	Period 1^{90}	Period 2^{90}
Period 2		
Period 3	Period 3^{45}	Period 3^{45}
Period 6	Period 6^{90}	Period 7^{90}
Period 7		

Table 5.14 Providing Project or Independent Study Time

	1		2		3			4	
	A	B	A	B	A	B	C	A	B
English	01	02	03	04	Lunch	Team meeting	Plan	Project	Time
Social Studies	01	02	03	04	Lunch	Team meeting	Plan	Project	Time
Math	Alg 01	Alg 02	PreAlg 01	PreAlg 02	Lunch	Team meeting	Plan	Project	Time
Science	01	02	03	04	Lunch	Team meeting	Plan	Project	Time
Special Education	Repl. Math	Repl. Eng	In-class support	In-class support	Lunch	Team meeting	Plan	Project	Time

grouping should not persist throughout the year, some instruction merits various groupings of students within the classroom of a small learning community. Kagan (1994) suggests four different types of groups: heterogeneous, random, interest, and homogeneous language. Each form meets a different learning need of the students involved (p. 6:1). These groups change to fit the format necessary to address their point of readiness and meet the learning target (Tomlinson, 1999).

Other opportunities for grouping and regrouping occur when necessary to move the student from the assigned classroom to another class or classroom: reassigning students from one teaching section of a team to another section of that interdisciplinary team; regrouping students in a single-subject foreign language team based on student performance on surveys, pretests, and/or posttests; offering students a choice of electives for a segment of the physical education course; and regrouping students based upon progress demonstrated in specific skill areas of the reading/language arts or mathematics curriculum.

Project or independent study time allows the student to be engaged in personalized learning. Table 5.14 illustrates the flexibility available for project time. In the flexed schedule, students see each core teacher for 40 minutes at the outset of the school day. At the end of the day, students devote 90 minutes to a project, independent study experience, or interdisciplinary project.

SUMMARY

Small learning communities have three major tasks: responding to student needs, integrating and delivering the curriculum, and flexing time. Since the three tasks are interwoven, teams best address them through dialogue. Within the dialogue, new areas of brain research with implications for the delivery of instruction need to be considered. To enhance team dialogue, professional development and administrative support are essential to help teachers move beyond the initial formation of a team. To enable these cohorts to develop a comprehensive, functioning collaborative model, goal setting will be addressed in the next two chapters.

A Guide for Collaborative Conversations

To set the stage for a fuller understanding of the role and function of a small learning community or team, the following questions serve as a guide:

Leader Questions

1. How will the unique role and function of a team or small learning community emerge in our school or district?

2. What training is necessary for teachers to succeed as members of a cohort group?

3. How will the effectiveness of teams or small learning communities be evaluated?

Teacher Questions

1. How will students benefit from the collaborative approach?

2. How will teachers benefit from the collaborative approach?

3. How will teachers be involved in planning and evaluating the staff development for small learning communities?

4. In what ways should the teacher evaluation instrument reflect the team process?

5. How will teams or small learning communities impact the culture of the school?

6

Elements of Teaming

A Goal-Setting Process for Curriculum and Instruction

Sustained change requires time. Recognizing that change is a process and not an event, experts caution against the quick-fix approach (Dolan, 1994; Erickson, 2001; Senge, 2000; Zmuda et al., 2004). They further warn that changing the structure alone does not bring an increase in student achievement; instructional practices must change as well. In order to impact student achievement, Jackson urges the creation and implementation of more current forms of instruction to accompany any structural changes (Norton, 2000). Additionally, Felner et al. (1997) note the need for time to impact change: High-functioning schools that experienced increased student achievement implemented a *Turning Points* model over a period of time. The NASSP authors encourage principals to find creative ways to allocate time for staff collaboration on change (2004, 2006). These observations correlate with the systems approach discussed in Chapter 1.

Time, also, becomes a factor in the advice of Michael Fullan (2000), an expert on the change process, who suggests that a faculty, depending on school size and type, will take three to six years to implement all aspects of change. He fears, however, that progress will be short-lived if the changes are not institutionalized. A part of the move toward institutionalization occurs when change initiatives arise from teachers' classroom experiences. When those experiences are shared in what Fullan refers to as an inside-out reciprocity, a bottom-up/top-down combination occurs. His vision includes a focused and specific set of goals determined by those within the school who are "challenged and nurtured by an external infrastructure."

Fullan's remarks advance the importance of learning communities within the school, cohorts of teachers who meet and collaborate on pedagogy and assessment practices to meet the needs of their students. Senge et al. (2000) assert that strong professional communities work toward collective endeavors rather than individual ones. They cite Kruse, Louis, and Byrk, who, they note, encourage the development of a collaborative identity that promotes teacher empowerment: "Teachers with more discretion to make decisions regarding their work [tend to] feel more responsible for how well their students learn. . . . Instead of being guided by [imposed] rules, they are guided by the norms and beliefs of the professional community" (p. 331). As a result, teacher ownership of the program to be implemented increases.

To empower teachers and to affect student learning, it is necessary to set goals. The agreed-upon goals must be reasonable in number to avoid the "initiative overload" often experienced by teachers. If specific goals are not identified and the team's work remains unfocused, fragmentation, the other foe of "reculturing," occurs (Fullan, 2000). Ideally, in order to build ownership, cohort groups should select their goals based on the needs of their students, the requirements of the school, and the expectations created by national, state, and district standards. Although an established small learning community is likely to have some aspects of the goals in place, full implementation of the SLC role and function occurs when all goal elements are operational.

This chapter presents goals in four areas that are fundamental to implementing the role and function of a team. Chapter 7 addresses the goal-setting process for practical organizational considerations. Choosing from the lists in both chapters, teams should limit the number of goals on which to focus for a year to avoid overload and fragmentation. Given their lack of experience in collaboration, newly formed cohorts need even more care to choose types and numbers of goals that can be achieved. Three or four choices per year are reasonable; several should be selected from the following four areas that reflect the role and function of a team:

- Response to student needs
- Curriculum integration and delivery
- Academic planning
- Flexible/creative uses of time

To sustain the chosen initiatives, schools and districts provide professional development support to houses, small learning communities, and magnets for the specific goals selected. The support needs to be focused and not fragmented in the manner of the frequently-offered buffet type of workshop on professional days. Focused support includes a follow-up component for ongoing reflection and redirection. As each goal is identified in this chapter, specific examples for implementation are presented. Cohort groups choose from the menu according to their strengths, interests, and uniqueness.

RESPONSE TO STUDENT NEEDS

In any cohort group, students wear many guises, lacking uniformity within or across teams. Consequently, teams endeavor to find creative ways to respond to the group of students or an individual student within the group. The authors of *Breaking Ranks II* emphasize the importance of meeting student needs by citing DiMartino (2001, p. 19): "Reaching all students depends on reaching each one" (NASSP, 2004). Personalized instruction discussed in *Breaking Ranks* and *Turning Points 2000* suggests the use of learning modalities and appropriate levels of abstraction. Teams and teachers who set goals that focus on learning styles develop lessons or activities that build on auditory, verbal, or kinesthetic strengths. Additional lesson cohesiveness occurs when teachers provide continuity in concept development by sequencing concrete to abstract activities.

By choosing goals that focus on a collaborative approach to meeting student needs, teachers create a greater impact on instruction. Several ideas for goal implementation follow:

- Arrange for frequent meetings with the school counselor(s) to review cumulative records, standardized test scores, academic records, and other data.
- Record anecdotal notes about students that form a profile of the typical seventh- or ninth-grade student in terms of intellectual/cognitive and/ or social-emotional development.
- Invite the school psychologist or social worker to team meetings to discuss students in general, students in particular, or issues such as peer pressure, the search for sophistication, or some aspect of career development.
- Attend lectures or seminars on adolescent behavior and identify strategies to implement ideas offered by speakers.
- Survey students and parents to learn more about student development, interest in community issues, or dynamics within the school community.
- Create a database on student achievement (reading scores, mathematics scores, or other state, national, and local assessments) and monitor progress throughout the year.
- Plan lessons or activities as a team to reinforce students' strengths or needs.
- Create a unified discipline code for the academy or house in light of students' developmental needs, including social-emotional and moral development.
- Study and implement student-led conferences.

The use of these activities promotes a better understanding of students' needs and incorporates the power of a team response.

CURRICULUM INTEGRATION AND DELIVERY

The team or small learning community structure provides unique opportunities to collaborate on curriculum integration and delivery. Because learning is enhanced when students recognize patterns and relationships, integration has become the foundation of magnet and academy experiences. Interdisciplinary approaches relevant to the needs of adolescent youth and reflective of real-world experiences weave the fabric of student engagement.

An art exists in the process of implementing curriculum integration and delivery. Working together, teams or small learning communities learn that art. They come to understand when integration should take place, which disciplines are to be involved, and what is the process for developing the intended instruction (Erickson, 2001). In addition to the suggestions offered in Chapter 5, the following strategies are suggested to phase in this element of collaboration.

Curriculum mapping provides a process as proposed by Heidi Hayes-Jacobs (2004) for continual review of curriculum, assessment, and monitoring of student improvement. The year's vision of the curriculum influences the decisions made for the creation of the weekly plan chart, one guiding the other. Discussion and a prototype to implement curriculum mapping are found in Chapter 5.

Weekly plan charts identify areas available for integration, including attention to the vocabulary used in each area. During the team meeting dedicated to the weekly plan chart as noted in Table 6.1, each teacher discusses the learning goals, activities, and assessments for the following week. If possible, encore, exploratory, and/or elective subjects should be included as well. At this time, coordination of assessment and projects takes place so that students can pace their study-time attention. During the week, as formative assessment takes place within each class, any need for changes to the weekly plan chart can be discussed and altered.

Table 6.1   Weekly Plan Chart: Concept, Strategy, Skill

Concept: Strategy: Skill-of-the-week:					
WEEK:	*Monday*	*Tuesday*	*Wednesday*	*Thursday*	*Friday*
Language Arts					
Literature/Reading					
Spelling/Vocabulary					
Mathematics					
Science					
Social Studies					
(Other)					
Advisory					
Special Activities/Plans					

Skill-of-the-week pertains to the choice of a basic or thinking skill that guides and integrates instructional delivery. These skill choices enhance the weekly curriculum plan. To provide a clear understanding, the specific models presented in Chapter 5, Tables 5.8 and 5.9, can be expanded or revised to meet standard and curriculum needs.

Strategies for curriculum delivery are geared to the needs of the students. The strength of the team relies upon the members' experiences and expertise in the area of instructional strategies that focus on student success. Team time needs to be spent discussing topics such as cooperative learning, learning styles, differentiation of instruction, and implications of brain research. By following their discussions with implementation, teachers ensure success.

ACADEMIC PLANNING

To facilitate student achievement, comprehensive academic planning is essential and becomes a major responsibility of teams, small learning communities, magnets, houses, or academies. Within the broad category of academic planning, two major subcategories exist: long-term and short-term goals. Each goal begins its existence in one of the planning formats previously discussed: curriculum mapping, weekly plan chart, or skill-of-the-week.

Long-Term Goals

Long-term goals contribute to the fulfillment of a team's vision. The content of the goals arises from the purpose identified by the team and the composite skills and interests of the team members. Senge et al. (2000) encourage members to recognize the creative or structural tension that exists between goals and current reality. Disciplined movement toward these goals includes review, evaluation, persistence, and revision. Without these steps, the gap between achieving the goal and maintaining the status quo remains. To help autonomous teams achieve their goals, principals play important roles as facilitators (Jackson & Davis, 2000).

At the beginning of an academic year, the team needs to identify a specific time in the agenda for the week to discuss and begin to implement the chosen goals. The focus of long-term goals lies in exploring specific student needs, curriculum maps, state and national standards, and/or the team's mission. At this time, teams may choose a concept focus for instruction. A concept focus moves beyond a more specific topic and provides the broad understanding that will advance curriculum integration (Erickson, 2001; Tomlinson, 1999; Wiggins & McTighe, 1998). Through purposeful discussion, timely and constructive planning takes place. The following examples reflect both cognitive and affective topics:

- Facilitate transition of students from elementary to middle school.
- Facilitate transition of students from middle to high school.
- Orient students to careers in health.
- Prepare high school students for beginning jobs in the field of technology.

- Deliver an interdisciplinary unit entitled "Change" for eighth-grade students.
- Enable tenth graders to see the relationship between the animation magnet curriculum and the scope and sequence of English 10 and World Studies 10.

Short-Term Goals

Short-term goals, a set of more immediate goals, are crafted by a group of teachers once long-term goals are in place. Short-term goals guide instruction for the small learning community and subject areas for a week, month, or quarter of the school year. In order for these goals to be effective, they, too, need to be broken into their component parts.

For example, a long-term goal might include an interdisciplinary unit for eighth-grade students entitled *Change.* Within the unit, the entire team may focus on identified short-term goals such as the following:

- History of change from 1950 to 2000
- Examples of change as presented in novels
- Relationship of technology to the quality of life in American society
- Examples of art and music that impact the culture of American society

Within those short-term goal topics, learning engagements focus on the specific skill or content to be learned. For instance, when studying the history of change from 1950 to 2000, students work on compare/contrast analysis by researching arenas of change according to different content areas, such as countries, law, dress, sports, or science discoveries. By incorporating the information into several content areas, teachers provide the repetition necessary to place it into long-term memory.

As with content, students require opportunities for repeated skills practice in order to secure skills in long-term memory. Similarly, skills need to be scaffolded for ease of understanding and formative assessment. The resulting incremental steps aid in the process of formative assessment so that the pacing of instruction may be altered as needed. Ideas for targeted skills include:

- Reading for main ideas
- Narrative writing skills
- Identification of theme
- Use of timeline
- Use of charts and graphs
- Probability and statistics
- Use of graphing calculator
- Data analysis
- Noting changes in perspective
- Rhythm

While some teachers identify short-term goals within long-term goals, others may identify long-term goals from a listing of short-term goals. In either case, it is essential to work with both long- and short-term goals in academic planning. As with other areas of educational restructuring, these elements do not happen by accident but are the result of collegial discussion and instructional commitment.

Plans for the first day, first week, and first month of the school year establish a balance between the emphasis on the small learning community and the focus on individual subjects. To allow teachers time to focus on developing the delivery of their individual curriculum and to plan how to incorporate team decisions into the content areas, team protocols need to be established early. Through discussion, members decide a variety of team coordination issues, e.g., decision-making format, team/classroom rules, discipline policy, common procedures such as manuscript form, parent contact procedures, student responsibilities, and team identity activities (George & Alexander, 1993; Merenbloom, 1991; Stevenson, 1998). The organizational decisions characterize each team and allow the identity of the team to emerge. Stronge (2002) suggests that the use of established procedures and structures maximizes instructional time by eliminating student down-time. Further, students need to be aware of the teacher's commitment to team and subject area.

In order to provide a smooth beginning to the school year, team planning meetings are needed prior to the students' arrival. These meetings focus on plans for the students' first day, week, and month including methods to make students aware of the team protocols. Once protocols are identified, the team members continue toward content area orientation and begin to achieve the team's goals. Table 6.2 presents a visual to help team members plan for this balance. The chart can be recreated on computer to provide a fluid plan that can be easily modified.

Plans for this week, this month, and next month help the team members to be sensitive to their vision of long- and short-term goals. While the weekly plan chart enables the team to monitor and plan instruction for the week, Table 6.3 can be used to plan for a two-month period. Like other charts presented, Table 6.3 works well when recreated on the computer. Whether using the weekly plan chart; the first day, week, and month chart; or the week, month, two-month chart, teachers need to refer consistently to the curriculum map to monitor the relationship between long- and short-term goals. This process impacts the small learning community as well as each content area in the cohort group.

Table 6.2   Plans for the First Day, First Week, and First Month

	Team Focus	*Activities for Team Focus*	*Activities for Content Area*
First Day			
First Week			
First Month			

Table 6.3   Plans for This Week, This Month, and Next Month

	Team Focus	Activities for Team Focus	Activities for Content Area
This Week			
This Month			
Next Month			

Connections of the planning period and agenda to the instructional program are vital to consistency and continuity. Effective teachers understand the relationship between planning periods and the instructional program. Just as time presents itself as an important factor in the classroom delivery of instruction, the manner in which time is used in planning periods separates the highly functioning team from the lesser functioning team (Stevenson, 1998). During the team meeting, the amount of time focused on instruction must surpass the amount of time spent on discussions of student behavior (Jackson & Davis, 2000). When the focus on instruction becomes the paramount consideration in meetings, the team begins to visualize the interwoven nature of the subjects represented (Capelluti & Brazee, 2003).

Agendas are important to make and keep in order to maintain the team's focus. Through adherence to the agenda and purposeful discussion of the agenda's items, a strong instructional program and a cohesive, high-performing team emerge. That cohesiveness is enhanced when each member has a voice in creating the agenda. Suggestions for the agenda follow:

- Develop an agenda for each team meeting with a follow-up column to list anticipated actions or to note actions that have already occurred.
- Create a guideline so that at least one agenda item of each meeting will focus on academic planning.
- Focus regularly on long- and/or short-term goals of the small learning community as well as individual subjects.
- Encourage all members to add agenda items.
- Provide an opportunity for periodic team evaluations. Team members should be prepared to document/support their responses using the following questions:
  - To what extent do we as a team see the relationship between planning periods and the instructional program?
  - To what extent do team members make the connection between the agenda and the instructional program?
  - In what ways do team members take decisions made by the team and apply them to their classroom?

Because academic planning is a major element of teaming, SLCs must eventually implement the identified goals in an integrated fashion.

FLEXIBLE AND CREATIVE USES OF TIME

The concept of flexibility is applicable to small learning communities that utilize specific structural options: interdisciplinary–maximum flexibility, inter-disciplinary-encore/exploratory, or combination teams. With this opportunity for flexibility, teams may choose to alter the sequence of classes, arrange large group instruction, extend or reduce time periods, regroup students, and/or allocate project time.

Cohorts of teachers can implement the following flexible and creative uses of time:

- Ascertain similarities of the schedules of each teacher to determine the basis for flexibility.
- Identify the theoretical and practical parameters of altered sequence, large group, extended/reduced time, regrouping, and/or project time in terms of the teaching and learning process.
- Select one option for flexibility and organize a pilot effort for implementation. Evaluate the pros and cons of the pilot effort.
- Keep anecdotal records of experiences where flexibility was implemented. Note comments of students and teachers, evidence of student success and achievement, impact on faculty, and impact student morale.
- Create a team policy to implement and sustain flexibility.
- In light of the team's experiences and experimentation with flexibility, offer suggestions to the administration to improve the master schedule for the next school year.

Chapter 2 provides a more in-depth discussion of structural options that provide opportunities for flexibility.

SUMMARY

Implementing the role and function of a team involves a series of steps that evolve into a series of goals. This chapter presents four major goal areas with some areas containing subgoals. Additional suggestions on organizational considerations appear in Chapter 7. Recognizing that change is a process that requires incremental steps, teams or small learning communities need to create a timetable of three to six years for full implementation of the goals.

A Guide for Collaborative Conversations

To set the stage for a fuller understanding of the goal-setting process, the following questions, which focus on implementing the role and function of a team or small learning community, serve as a guide to achieving a direct impact on curriculum and instruction:

Leader Questions

1. How will the school/district introduce the goal-setting process?

2. How will teachers begin to see the relationship between the initial four goal areas and the ultimate role or function of a team or small learning community?

3. What process will be used to enable cohorts of teachers to inventory their strengths and limitations regarding the team's role and function?

4. What staff development resources will be available to help teachers achieve goals they have selected?

Teacher Questions

1. How will we select our goals to phase in the comprehensive role and function of a team?

2. How many goals can be reasonably accomplished for the first year? How many can be reasonably accomplished in successive years?

3. What resources will be available as we pursue our goals related to establishing the role and function of a team?

4. How will this goal-setting process be evaluated?

Elements of Teaming

A Goal-Setting Process
for Organizational Considerations

While Chapter 6 focuses on elements of the role and function of a team that directly affect curriculum and instruction, Chapter 7 presents the practical, organizational aspects of teaming. These decisions provide a foundation for consistency within the team. Through the gradual incorporation of these practical goals, cohort groups add to the framework by which teams measure progress. Further, by putting the organizational elements in place, the team frees time to focus on instruction and its delivery (Brown, K. M., 2001; George & Alexander, 1993). Remembering Fullan's admonition (1982, cited in Marzano, 2003, p. 159) to take small steps to reach large goals, team members need to prioritize their organizational needs. Eight elements of practical consideration follow:

1. Inclusion or mainstreaming of special needs students

2. Team-building process

3. Team meetings

4. Discipline protocols

5. Team leaders

6. Team evaluations

7. Conflict resolution

8. Parental contact and involvement

By choosing reasonably achievable goals from Chapters 6 and 7, teams increase their ability to succeed. As presented in Chapter 6, team member interests, prior experiences, and personal philosophies determine selections. Within three to six years, all twelve elements can be in place.

INCLUSION OR MAINSTREAMING OF SPECIAL NEEDS STUDENTS

According to Rebecca A. Hines (2001), the concept of inclusion exists in law but the term inclusion does not appear in any legislation, and its definition varies from district to district. Most often, its use refers to students with disabilities. The term differs from mainstreaming in that inclusion students belong primarily to general education classes and not to a separate instructional environment. Many teachers, however, refer to special needs students as inclusion students (Wang & Reynolds, 1997).

Wherever possible, the special education staff member is a member of the interdisciplinary team. Research indicates that students identified as special needs students perform most successfully when in a combination program of regular classroom and resource room support (Holloway, 2001).

Team meetings provide an excellent opportunity for regular education and special education teachers to share ideas about instruction and classroom management. Several factors impact special needs students and must be considered by the entire team to implement the goal:

- State and national laws regarding the placement of special needs students
- The content of each Individual Educational Program (IEP) for specific students assigned to the team, house, magnet, small learning community, or academy
- The role of resource and support personnel within the regular classroom
- Strategies that are research-supported for special needs students
- Learning modalities, multiple intelligences, and methods to differentiate instruction for both regular and special education students
- Strategies to monitor performance of special needs students
- Remediation and enrichment techniques
- Ongoing assessment of student and program successes

When the above elements are considered, discussed, and implemented as needed by the team, special needs students experience the benefits of effective instruction. The students then become fully included within the small learning community.

TEAM-BUILDING PROCESS

From inception, teams need time, motivation, and opportunities to bond. In order to develop their specific sense of community, teams need to engage in a series of team-building activities (George & Alexander, 1993; Merenbloom, 1991). They further enable a school to provide personalization practices to set the stage for learning (NASSP, 2004, 2006). Decisions that address the team's practical operations affect the team's culture, an essential ingredient for institutionalizing change (McAdams, 1997). Therefore, to facilitate the establishment of a team's culture, teams need to implement team-building activities prior to the beginning of a new school year or, at the latest, early during the first marking period.

To implement team building, the following seven dimensions, presented in Tables 7.1 through 7.7, guide the process. They are best implemented when members complete responses individually before sharing with colleagues. Ideas that arise from the discussion help to provide an atmosphere for open dialogue and building community.

Table 7.1   Getting to Know Each Other

Question	Response
1. What are your hobbies or special interests?	
2. What are your feelings about being a member of this small learning community?	
3. What strengths do you bring to the small learning community?	
4. In what ways can the team support you?	

Table 7.2   Expectations of Other Team Members

Question	Response
1. How can team members collaborate regarding discipline problems?	
2. How will members of a small learning community identify team goals?	
3. How can teachers of a team be a support system for each other?	

Table 7.3   Expectations of Resource Personnel

Question	Response
1. Who are the resource personnel available to our cohort group?	
2. How often should the school counselor attend team meetings?	
3. How often should school administrators attend team meetings?	
4. How often should other resource personnel attend team meetings?	
5. In what ways can resource personnel help the small learning community accomplish its goals?	

Table 7.4   Procedures to Establish Team Goals

Question	Response
1. What topics or concerns represent possible long- or short-term team goals?	
2. What factors influence goal selection?	
3. How will goal achievement be assessed?	

Table 7.5   Expectations of the Team Leader

Question	Response
1. What is the main responsibility of the team leader?	
2. In what ways can team members support the team leader?	
3. What should the team leader do when there is a deadlock on a particular issue?	
4. What strategies keep members focused on agenda items?	
5. What should occur when members do not participate or fulfill their team roles?	
6. What is the relationship between the team leader and the principal?	

Table 7.6   Consensus Needed for Team Decisions

Question	Response
1. What will constitute consensus for a decision?	
2. What should occur when teams cannot reach consensus?	
3. How will the team respond when a member does not support a specific decision?	

Table 7.7   Curriculum Mapping

Question	Response
1. When will the curriculum map be completed?	
2. What subjects should be included on the curriculum map?	
3. How will communication flow between small learning community members and other teachers?	
4. How will the curriculum map be used to integrate instruction?	
5. How will the team evaluate the utilization of the curriculum map?	

TEAM MEETINGS

In order to maximize planning time, teachers need significant professional development to learn how to conduct productive team meetings. Newly formed teams as well as experienced teams improve the productivity of meetings by developing an agenda, examining the role responsibility of each team member, maintaining a record of team decisions, and utilizing subgroupings when appropriate. Primarily, efficient meetings focus on elements of instruction rather than issues with students (Ames, 2004; Hackmann et al., 2002; Jackson & Davis, 2000).

Agenda

The agenda provides structure for team meetings with a focus for the week as well as a focus for the day. By designating a specific target for various days of the week, teams maintain an efficient format to address their essential

Table 7.8   Team 6A, Monday: Student Concerns

Team 6A
• Reading group assignment change for two students
• School nurse discusses two students with health problems
• Referral of student for special services
• Discussion of returned homework sheets
• Evaluation of orientation program

Table 7.9   Team 8A, Tuesday: Curriculum

Team 8A
• Final draft of curriculum map
• Review data from reading assessment
• Review plans for team science field trip
• Plans for schedule adjustment: extend periods
• Plans for skill-of-the-week: cause-and-effect relationships

Table 7.10   Team 9C, Thursday: Support Personnel

Team 9C
• Counselor visit to discuss advisory program on study skills
• Psychologist visit to discuss confidential report
• Principal visit to discuss parent open house

Table 7.11   Animation Magnet, Friday: Curriculum

Animation Magnet
• Curriculum map discussion: connections between English 10, World History, and Animation II
• Review of student Individual Education Program (IEP)
• Follow-up discussion on cooperative learning strategies
• Plans for Web page section on curriculum

component parts: curriculum, weekly plan chart, short- and long-range goals, professional growth topics, student concerns, and meetings with support personnel. In turn, these topics determine the agenda for the day.

Although each team member should have input into developing the agenda, care needs to be taken to limit the discussion of each topic to a reasonable amount of time. Further, a balance must exist between the three domains of teaming: responding to student needs, curriculum delivery and integration, and flexible/creative uses of time. By using the agenda, team members allow the true culture of the team to emerge (Dolan, 1994).

Team Member Responsibilities

Team member responsibilities must be adhered to for the team process to function in the most effective and efficient manner. To help team members fulfill their role responsibility, six suggestions follow:

1. *Accept team placement.* Teachers may or may not have a voice in choosing other members of the cohort group. Successful collaboration, however, requires skill in social interactions (Brown, K. M., 2001). Consequently, acceptance of team assignment and colleagues reflects the professionalism of the members involved and sets a tone for the entire team. To establish this mindset, teams need adequate staff development (Erb & Doda, 1989, cited by Brown, K. M., 2001).

2. *Promote exploration of the topic.* Complexity defines the world inhabited by the students of today. That complexity requires thoughtful approaches to topics and themes of instruction or team protocols. Consequently, when discussing elements of curriculum or team organization, successful team members actively work to explore all aspects of a topic. The use of open-ended questions facilitates exploration and curtails a single member's dominance. When engaged in true dialogue, participants "pay attention to the spaces between the words" as well as the words and "suspend their assumptions," looking at them from different perspectives (Senge et al., 2000, p. 75). After all team members contribute to a comprehensive exploration of the issue, consensus can be achieved.

3. *Be honest in all communications.* When cohort members share a mission, they are better able to be honest with each other. An atmosphere of honesty reflects the positive interrelationships that exist within the team, which K. M. Brown refers to as an atmosphere of regard (2001, p. 56). If each member puts into practice the use of open and frank answers and comments, trust becomes a part of the team culture. To the extent possible, team members should understand what other colleagues believe on an issue, to practice what Dolan (1994) calls "grace" and understanding of each person's struggle with change (p. 166). While varied points of view are encouraged, disagreements need to be aired within the team with grace.

4. *Use the listening technique of reflection.* Excellent teachers possess a keen understanding of their craft, which they continue to perfect through

personal reflection (Senge et al., 2000). Some of that reflection is stimulated by conversations within the team through focused listening, an important aspect of dialogue. Because a good group member is a good listener, the listener helps the speaker to clarify a thought. In response to that thought, the listener causes other members to reflect by paraphrasing statements and identifying related feelings. The response "you really disagree with us on that matter, but you are reluctant to say so" is an example of reflection. In this example, both content (facts) and affect (feelings) are being reflected. *Content* is a summary of what is being discussed while *affect* describes feelings or emotions associated with facts. A good listener reflects both *content* and *affect* (Merenbloom, 1991).

5. *Nonverbal cues should be monitored.* Besides the use of productive dialogue, nonverbal communication affects the meeting atmosphere (George & Alexander, 1993). Members of a small learning community should be keenly aware of nonverbal messages sent out as they talk to colleagues, resource persons, parents, students, or others attending meetings. Verbal statements taken alone may mislead participants or attendees. Depending on timing, content of the verbal discussion, or personality of the speaker, a particular gesture may have varied meanings. By paying attention to nonverbal cues, the participant gains additional understanding of a person as well as the message being delivered.

6. *Recognize the relationship between the small learning community, the school, and the school system.* Successful teams efficiently use their autonomy. Without a sense of community and strong leadership to encourage that sense of community, teams can abuse their autonomy. Just as individual teachers find comfort in what Dolan (1994) describes as the "cult of the individual," teams can assume the same mentality (p. 82). In this mode, systemic change and wellbeing are sacrificed for isolated comfort. Further, this isolated mode of thinking encourages competition instead of collaboration with other teams, the school, and the district. Besides adhering to rules and guidelines of the school and school system, leaders and teams can foster cooperation by recognizing the accomplishments of all teams and communicating in regularly scheduled grade-level meetings (Ames & Miller, 1994, cited in Brown, K. M., 2001, p. 50). Planning then becomes more comprehensive and provides a more consistent student educational experience.

Record of Team Decisions

The record of team decisions maintained throughout the school year enhances team effectiveness. According to Erb and Doda (1989), failure to do so represents one of the problems that makes teaming difficult (cited by Brown, K. M., 2001, p. 50). The team agenda helps to identify the items for the record; other items include parent contacts, involvement of support personnel, and team role responsibilities. Although the team can develop its own format, Tables 7.12 and 7.13 offer suggestions. In Table 7.12, the agenda is structured with entries made within categories. Teams monitor the extent to which they are addressing each category.

Table 7.12   Team Planning Log, Sample A

Team, Small Learning Community, or Magnet:	
Goal(s):	
Date:	
Focus Areas	*Actions*
Content	
Skill Development	
Applications to Real Life	
Pupil Adjustment Issues	
Team Goal Accomplishments	
Other	

In Table 7.13, categories reinforce the three domains of the role and function of a team or small learning community: responding to student needs, curriculum integration and delivery, and creative/flexible uses of time. The fourth section remains open for miscellaneous entries. Teams record discussions or agenda items in the designated or appropriate space. As a result, team members are able to see teaming in a holistic fashion.

Table 7.13   Planning Log, Sample B

Team, Small Learning Community, or Magnet:	
Goal(s):	
Date:	
1. Response to Student Needs	2. Curriculum Integration and Delivery
3. Flexible/Creative Uses of Time	4. Other

Periodically, as part of their team evaluation, teams should pause and reflect upon records of team decisions accumulated over a period of time. By tallying the frequency of entries in a category or merely reflecting upon the content of the reports, teachers begin to assess team effectiveness, priorities, or successes.

Team or SLC Subgroups

When necessary, subgroups of the team or SLC can address a specific issue or other item of team business. Prior to the subgroup meeting, the full team agrees to items assigned to the subgroup; decisions of subgroups require team approval. Examples of subgroup assignments include the following:

- Coordinating plans for field trips
- Coordinating plans for assemblies and guest speakers
- Planning by pairs of English and social studies teachers
- Planning by pairs of mathematics and science teachers
- Coordinating advisory program
- Gathering input for curriculum maps
- Developing yearly schedule for skill-of-the-week
- Publishing team newsletter
- Revising Web page
- Scheduling new or follow-up parent conferences

Subgroups utilize the strengths of cohort members and enable them to make productive use of available planning time.

ESTABLISHING A DISCIPLINE CODE

The developmental needs of adolescent students require consistency, a part of which includes discipline. Too often, however, the topic of discipline invokes adult behaviors and attitudes of control and punishment, promoting the normal adolescent sense of rebellion. Rather than control and punishment, the goal of discipline should be to encourage a sense of responsibility and to increase opportunities for the school to create a safe and orderly environment.

Both Marzano (2003) and the authors of *Breaking Ranks* (NASSP, 1996) emphasize the need to establish an environment in which teaching and learning can safely take place. Marzano lists "a safe and orderly environment" as one of the essential school-level factors that affect student achievement (p. 53). Further, school safety continually arises on surveys as a chief concern of parents. This fact may be due to the extensive media coverage of particularly violent events in schools. To refute that impression, Marzano cites Noguera (1995) in explaining that students may be more safe in school than in other areas they may frequent (p. 54).

Through their collective decision-making roles as part of team policy, teams may allay many parental and societal concerns. In the area of discipline, they establish consistency by formulating and implementing a discipline policy that facilitates learning and respects the dignity of students. Team decisions have the advantage of being more broad-based, articulated, and implemented than those of an individual teacher. The development of a simple but firm discipline code should contain few rules that are equitably enforced. All team members participate in formulating the rules, presenting the guidelines, and informing students of the consequences of violating the rules.

The enforcement of the rules cannot be arbitrary and must be consistently applied by each member of the team. Although a variety of strategies can be used to implement the rules, all strategies need to maintain an atmosphere of respect for the student. In fact, team cohesiveness and overt concern for the students often promote a higher level of behavior than might be seen in individual classrooms (George & Alexander, 1993). Ultimately, the goal of a safe and orderly environment for teaching and learning leads the team to their decisions for discipline. Possible strategies to be considered in implementing this goal include the following:

- Provide positive recognition for student successes.
- Invite the student to discuss the problem with team members and collaboratively establish goals for improvement.
- Invite the school counselor or building administrator to join the teachers to discuss a student problem.
- Invite parents to team meetings to inform them of a problem and/or solicit their assistance before a situation is beyond control.
- Utilize the expertise of the school social worker and psychologist.
- Develop an Individualized Student Plan (ISP) to correct a problem by utilizing the strengths of team members.
- Determine if a change of teaching section within the small learning community would benefit the student.

TEAM LEADERS

The team leader facilitates the emergence of the team's personality, capitalizes on the members' strengths, and leads them without fanfare into becoming a cohesive learning organization in which all members can contribute and grow (Senge, 1990). No other cohort group within the school organization has the same teachers, same students, or, in some magnet cases, the same curriculum. Through the efforts of team leaders, each cohort group develops its own organization to accomplish its goals, vision, and purposes. As a result, each small learning community has its measure of local autonomy, opportunities for decision making, and/or governance. Through the members' ability to govern themselves, they collaboratively build ownership (Jackson & Davis, 2000).

The successful team leader serves as a catalyst to enable the group to achieve its full potential as an independent organism. External sources cannot and should not provide the leadership needed for the day-to-day functioning of each team. Any top-down control destroys the team's sense of autonomy, responsibility, and collective vision. Although one person fulfills the leadership role, all members accept responsibility for this function. Further, in order for all members to develop the special form of leadership required in a collaborative effort, the position of team leader should be rotated each quarter, semester, year, or two years (Jackson & Davis, 2000).

The responsibilities of the leader can be divided into three segments: implementing the role and function of a team, facilitating and coordinating team functions, and completing managerial or administrative tasks. Each category contains numerous opportunities for leadership and must be phased in over time.

Implementing the role and function of a small learning community requires a more holistic view of the team process:

- Helping team members implement the vision, mission, or philosophy of the cohort
- Being certain that team members see the relationship between planning periods and instructional program

- Assisting team members in identifying creative ways to respond to students' unique needs
- Facilitating integration of the entire curriculum through assigning a member the role of curriculum coach
- Encouraging teachers to explore, utilize, and assess their successes with a variety of teaching and learning strategies
- Helping teachers utilize a variety of flexible scheduling and grouping strategies
- Developing strategies to integrate each domain of the role and function of a team
- Incorporating professional growth discussions during team meetings
- Ensuring collaboration with other teams and teachers of other subjects to avoid an attitude of isolation

Facilitating and coordinating team functions require insightful leadership qualities:

- Accepting all team members and support staff
- Providing team-building activities as needed
- Monitoring the effectiveness of decision-making processes within the team
- Involving all team members in discussions
- Verifying consensus
- Dealing with differences of opinion among team members
- Facilitating the evaluation of the team
- Monitoring the achievement of team goals

Completing managerial and administrative tasks entails a focus on the day-to-day issues:

- Presiding over meetings
- Developing an agenda for each meeting
- Providing assistance for substitute teachers
- Handling paperwork for the team or delegating that responsibility
- Coordinating planning for special events
- Serving as the liaison with the administration
- Meeting with the principal as requested or needed
- Submitting reports and receiving communications for the team
- Informing special area teachers of team activities
- Coordinating the involvement of resource personnel
- Utilizing subgroupings of the team when appropriate

It would be virtually impossible for a prospective team leader to master or try to implement all twenty-eight skills concurrently; consequently, teams should be realistic about the number of items they attempt to implement. In the goal-setting process, however, teams select items in each major category on an annual basis.

Although team leaders frequently do not receive training for their roles, they, like other team members, are in need of adequate preparation. Periodically, a feedback system should be employed to determine the success of meeting the leadership goals selected (Senge, 1990). At the beginning of subsequent school years, additional tasks can be selected until all leadership skills are operational. By focusing on a reasonable selection of tasks and collaboratively seeking to complete them, the leader's facilitating role ensures success.

TEAM EVALUATION

Professional growth includes the ongoing formative assessment of team progress. Senge (1990) suggests that critical reflection and feedback form a part of this assessment, cautioning against the effect of seeing what is desired to be seen, the "self-fulfilling prophecy" identified by Robert Merton (cited by Senge, 1990, p. 80). Senge defines productive feedback as a "reciprocal flow of influence," moving in two directions rather than linear (p. 75). By employing such an open form of assessment, teams enhance communication and team effectiveness.

The self-evaluation model allows team members to examine team progress: present practice, needed improvement, and priorities for that improvement. Just as a student's progress can be self-evaluated through the use of a guiding instrument, teachers are better able to focus on the team's attributes by using a guide. The self-evaluation instrument in Table 7.14 sets the stage for team discussion.

Teams select specific questions that are most meaningful to their goals and complete the evaluation during a team meeting or as homework. Whichever method is chosen, the completed survey becomes the focus of discussion on a team's agenda.

With the team leader facilitating the discussion phase, members of the team share their responses and identify areas of agreement and disagreement. Effective discussion requires that each member support answers with reasons. When team members cite evidence for answers, discussion often reveals factors more important to the team than knowing that all members checked the column "consistently."

Obviously, a diversity of responses is healthy. In answering the question, "Are team decisions implemented?" two members may say "frequently" while two members indicate "occasionally." Rather than trying to get one team member to change the response to reach a majority, it is more important to find out why members responded the way they did. The discussion provoked by this survey and the student survey in Table 7.15 identifies the team as one that seeks ongoing feedback as a basis for professional development.

To augment the team survey, a student survey conveys to the team the effectiveness of the year's curriculum delivery and team interaction. Given at the end of the year, the survey provides teams with results to be used as guides for planning activities and curriculum for the following year.

After reviewing the surveys, team members use the information garnered as a basis for evaluation of the previous year. From the evaluations, the curriculum map and strategies for delivery of instruction for the following year can be revised and/or developed.

Table 7.14   Evaluating the Effectiveness of the SLC or Team

		Consistently	Frequently	Rarely	Comment
1.	Do specific goals/objectives exist for the year?				
2.	Do members evaluate goals/objectives periodically?				
3.	Are SLC members aware of their role and function?				
4.	Has the team defined the role of the team leader?				
5.	Does the team respond to identified student needs?				
6.	Does the SLC collectively focus on student achievement?				
7.	Do students recognize the benefit of the collaborative approach to instruction?				
8.	Do cohort members discuss their commitment to the chosen team goals?				
9.	Do SLC members integrate content?				
10.	Do team members unify their efforts to teach skills?				
11.	Are skills taught in context?				
12.	Do teachers utilize opportunities to integrate standards-based content and skills?				
13.	Are discussions of teaching strategies listed on the meeting agenda?				
14.	Do team members identify opportunities to alter the basic schedule?				
15.	Do teachers utilize opportunities to group and regroup students for various instructional purposes?				
16.	Are schedule adjustments related to instructional strategies?				
17.	Does the SLC strive to include special needs students?				
18.	Are instructional strategies for special needs students listed on the meeting agenda?				
19.	As a result of team-building activities, do members know each other well?				
20.	Do members discuss their professional expectations of each other?				
21.	Do all members participate equally in decision making?				
22.	Are decisions implemented?				

Table 7.14   (Continued)

		Consistently	Frequently	Rarely	Comment
23.	Is a record made of decisions?				
24.	Has a discipline policy been implemented?				
25.	Have channels of communication been established with parents?				
26.	Has the SLC utilized the results of follow-up surveys for students and parents?				
27.	Does an agenda exist for each meeting?				
28.	Do the agenda items relate to the three domains of the role and function of the team/SLC?				
29.	Are meetings devoted primarily to team business?				
30.	Do cohort members accept responsibilities assigned to them?				
31.	Does the total cohort form subgroups when appropriate?				
32.	Do members offer support to the team leader?				
33.	Are leadership responsibilities shared?				
34.	Do team members individually establish long-term goals?				
35.	Do team members individually establish short-term goals?				
36.	Does the team establish long-term goals?				
37.	Does the team establish short-term goals?				
38.	Do SLC members recognize the relationship between planning periods and the instructional program?				
39.	Do members informally evaluate the team process?				
40.	Do constructive suggestions result from the formal evaluation process?				
41.	Are efforts made to resolve conflicts?				
42	Are parent conferences productive?				
43.	Do resource personnel join the team as needed for parent conferences?				

Table 7.15   Team Survey: Student Input

Directions:

- Listen as your teacher reads each question.

- Ask questions to clarify your understanding.

- Write your answers as specifically as you can. These can be in the form of notes rather than in complete sentences.

- Signatures are optional.

Questions:

- In your opinion, what makes an outstanding team of teachers? Think of the characteristics of any good and successful team: sports, community, friends.

- What teaching styles help you most to learn? Think of all your classes, required and elective. Different classes may require different styles. Be specific.

- What activities and strategies help you most to learn? This includes not only those that are fun, but those in which you have to put a lot of effort.

- Name three things that you have studied this year that you will remember for a long time; these can be units, facts, strategies, projects, or skills.

- What strategies helped you communicate to your teacher what you learned this year?

- In what ways did you grow and/or change as a learner this year?

- Reflect on your learning year by giving your teaching team specific advice for any units, activities, or strategies to repeat. Explain how this might be done.

CONFLICT RESOLUTION

The extensive communication, interaction, and collaboration integral to teams, houses, academies, and magnet programs create situations in which disagreement or conflicts may arise. Interpersonal differences can magnify and become intrusive if team members fail to build a professional working relationship (Stevenson, 1998). Sometimes teachers bring to the team their intuitively held beliefs, which they are unable to explain or defend but to which they feel committed. The guiding ideas of the team or school culture are not apparent or understandable by them (Senge et al., 2000).

Senge (1990) suggests that great teams do not hide their conflict but use it productively. Through the discussions that take place to work through the conflict, a collaborative vision emerges. Conversely, the teams that do not allow conflict to arise or tend to subvert it fail to grow professionally. According to Argyris (1985, cited in Senge, p. 254), defensive mental models prevent team members from distinguishing the negative impact the attitudes have on the forward progress of the team.

Because differences need to be resolved and decisions need to be collaborative, conflict resolution should be viewed as positive, developmental, and a productive means to an end (Merenbloom, 1991). Three case studies follow to illustrate conflicts and their resolution. After each case study, questions guide further discussion. Instead of specific answers to these questions, each anecdote includes key factors to be considered in helping the group resolve the conflict or potential conflict in a positive way.

Case Study #1

In a year of major restructuring at the district level, a number of middle-level teachers were given the opportunity to transfer to high schools. In this way, the school district facilitated the success of the newly created ninth-grade program as well as the continued success of the middle school concept. A mathematics teacher assigned to one of the Grade 8 teams lacked the seniority to obtain a high school position. The teacher's consequent anger caused a negative atmosphere during team meetings as reflected in statements such as "middle school students do not want to learn" and "middle school students do not appreciate my efforts." Although the teacher attended every team meeting, the teacher did not participate in discussing agenda items.

Guide Questions

1. How can the mathematics teacher be helped to accept the middle school assignment without creating additional defensiveness?

2. Specifically, how can some of the anger be sublimated into more positive directions?

In answering these questions, consider the individual's need for more information about the developmental nature of middle school students, the degree to which the teacher is trained in mathematics pedagogy, and the need to meet expectations in the culture of that school. Several of these factors may impact this individual, who may or may not respond to other team members reaching out to help. The resolution can only occur after the individual recognizes the anger, accepts the assignment, and establishes a goal to move forward.

Case Study #2

One member of a three-person cohort in Grade 10 emerges as a domineering personality who demonstrates a desire for complete control of the small learning community. Toward this end, the teacher volunteers to handle all tasks. Additionally, this person is the first to speak on topics and reacts vehemently to dissenting viewpoints.

Guide Questions

1. What might be the underlying reasons for the actions of this individual?

2. What strategies could be suggested to the other members of the SLC to minimize the effect of the domineering personality?

3. If all else fails, what actions should the other members take?

The above questions require the consideration of the personality needs of the domineering teacher. In many ways, these actions may be compensatory for attention or recognition not received elsewhere. It is possible that this individual wants to be promoted to a leadership position and sees SLC leadership as a means to that end. This individual may not be aware that successful leadership is invisible. Only when the individual recognizes that other SLC members can competently fulfill responsibilities can resolution of the conflict occur.

Case Study #3

Because of a reorganization of small learning communities in Grade 9, two veteran teachers who worked together previously find themselves teamed with teachers new to the building. Rather than trying to build unity among the four teachers, the two who worked together previously become a clique within the group. Through their statements and actions, it becomes apparent that they are more interested in their own ideas and needs than in the ideas and needs of the other team members.

Guide Questions

1. What kinds of team-building activities can create a bond among the four teachers?

2. How might the two novice teachers discuss their exclusion from the clique at an SLC meeting?

3. What opportunities could be created for each of the veteran teachers to work with each new teacher on a specific task?

4. How could the evaluation process ameliorate this problem?

5. At the end of the school year, what factors might the principal consider in keeping this cohort intact for the next school year?

The security needs of the veteran teachers must be considered as well as the possible insecurity of the newly assigned teachers. Team-building activities may or may not solve the problem. In reality, the insecurity of the veteran teachers may be greater than the insecurity of the new teachers. A key to success in this case may be pairing veteran and novice teachers as subgroups on specific tasks.

Conflicts among team members need to be resolved in a professional, supportive, and nurturing fashion. By focusing on group dynamics, communication skills, respect, acceptance, professionalism, a belief in the collaborative process, and time, teams can effectively resolve conflicts. The art of conflict resolution includes recognition of the right to disagree, openness to various points of view, consideration of possible consequences, review of alternatives, negotiation, and compromise.

PARENTAL CONTACT AND INVOLVEMENT

Parental involvement, a key to the learning process, is difficult to achieve in the secondary grades. As the student progresses through the school experience, parents become less inclined to be involved. Often parents do not feel as though their input or involvement is sought (NASSP, 1996).

Parents, however, are stakeholders in the education of their children. Marzano (2003) ranks parent involvement as the third element in importance that affects student achievement (p. 19). Increasingly, schools and districts include parents in conversations about school governance. In these conversations, care needs to be taken to include not only those parents who exhibit active involvement but also those parents who have not been involved in school. This kind of openness and welcome to all stakeholders increases the likelihood of building a sense of community and shared vision (Zmuda et al., 2004).

Recognizing the important role of parents in successful educational experiences for children, James Comer's model (1984, 1988, as cited in Marzano, 2003, pp. 50–51) for school reform incorporates three teams: School Planning and Management, Student and Staff, and Parent Teams. Two of the teams involve parents or community members. On the School Planning and Management Team, parents contribute to decisions regarding policies affecting curriculum, the school environment, staff development, the evaluation of schoolwide initiatives, and the coordination of school groups. The Parent Team focuses on ways parents can participate in the school: chaperoning, tutoring, serving as an aide, being a guest speaker, or filling other identified needs. The small learning community provides a venue in which these parents can feel they are an integral part of their child's education.

Without invading the teacher's areas of expertise, parents provide information about the effectiveness of instruction for their children and the extent to which the child can communicate about a subject. Besides being observers of the endeavors of the school and the effects of instruction on their child, parents support the school as stockholders as well as stakeholders. Dolan (1994) speaks of the parent as one whose financial support can no longer be taken for granted and who needs to understand the mission of the school and to experience involvement with the school.

On an ongoing basis, teachers in teams or SLCs encourage parental support and involvement by fully integrating parental engagement in the team process. To accomplish this goal, teams may choose from a variety of strategies including school or team orientation, parent communications, and conferences. Often parent involvement begins with an open house that orients parents to the many activities and purposes of the small learning communities. At this time, parents meet the teachers and may receive a team handbook. Additional parent contacts may occur during designated team planning time. To maximize the benefit of parent-teacher interactions, teachers request a developmental history of the student from the parents. That information, added to the teachers' expertise in student achievement and the impact of peers on the student, confirms the importance of a collaborative partnership.

Parent Communication

Parent communication, accomplished by newsletter, e-mail, or telephone, builds a strong sense of community that empowers successful teams. Parents become a part of the mix through frequent and meaningful communication. Today's technology allows more frequent communication as well as more specific and timely information. District and school Web sites with team links allow teams to post their weekly plans, notices, and team activities. On a designated day in the team's weekly agenda, teams enter Web site information. The responsibility for posting team information can be assumed by one of the team members on a yearly basis or by all of the team members on a rotating basis. In some cases, students can be given the responsibility for creating and posting the information.

In addition to the instructional information posted, teams often include teachers' backgrounds. Parents appreciate knowing the levels of expertise and areas of interest of their students' teachers. With the availability of this information, special connections between home, student, and school can occur, such as those based on an interest in particular hobbies or skills that are not school-related. In conjunction with the team's Web site, individual team members post weekly plans, learning goals, essential questions, test dates for their content areas, and timetables for long term projects.

Through the use of e-mail, teachers provide prompt response to parent questions and quickly inform parents of significant student successes or problems. The immediacy of e-mail thwarts the escalation of problems due to a time lapse or an inability to contact parents via telephone. Further, e-mail gives parents the opportunity to respond quickly, which take-home notices and flyers cannot by themselves achieve.

For schools or communities that have little access to technology, frequent newsletters fill the void. Newsletters contain the same types of information as the Web sites and provide a hard copy for "refrigerator posting." Students can be given the responsibility for creating the newsletter, giving them some ownership of the team's function.

At the beginning of the year, teachers welcome parents into the team by making phone calls to their advisory or home-base groups. From these phone calls, records begin that will aid in the personalization of the student's school experience. Although phone calls can continue through the year, they have a downside: Phone calls are labor- and time-intensive, with the information frequently being left as a voice-mail rather than yielding a more personal interaction.

Traditionally, high schools have provided little opportunity for parent involvement beyond open house nights. The authors of *Breaking Ranks* (NASSP, 1996) seek to raise an awareness in the education community that parents of high school students play as important a role in their student's education as those of elementary-school children. They cite evidence that links family involvement with positive student achievement (Grissmer, 1994) and encourage additional forms of outreach to parents.

Joyce L. Epstein (1986, cited in NASSP, 1996, p. 91) advises that "parental involvement is a manipulable variable that can be designed to increase school effectiveness and to improve students' success." According to the National Education Association (cited in Marzano, 2003, p. 48), the responsibility for the home-school connection lies with schools, not with parents; therefore, schools must take the initiative to establish protocols for ongoing communication with parents. Further, school communication with parents needs to occur throughout the child's educational experience and needs to be in the major languages of the school in order to bring about the desired level of effectiveness (Marzano, 2003, p. 49).

Parent Surveys

Parent surveys provide invaluable information to the team about their child: personal habits, interests, and the impact of instruction. When sent at the beginning of the school year and kept by the small learning community in the student's information folder, it becomes a point of reference whenever that information is needed. Table 7.16 provides a sample survey that requests parent observations and knowledge about the student's learning style, study habits, hobbies, and a brief summary of the child as seen through the parents' eyes. By color-coding the survey according to advisory or home-base classes, the teacher responsible for parent contacts is easily identified.

Later, at semester break, an additional parent survey can be sent home to provide the team with additional feedback. This survey seeks to know the skill level of the student in relation to homework assigned or level of understanding of directions given for assignments. Additional questions might relate to the accessibility of teachers, the grading system, or the timeliness of responses to parent concerns.

Because much of the response may be based on perception, teachers and teams need to put these responses in context and use them as part of a formative evaluation of interactions with the student (Danielson & McGreal, 2000). When the team makes the effort to maintain contact with parents and to seek input, opportunities for positive interaction and parental support increase.

Parent Conferences

Parent conferences present an ideal way to develop a personalized interaction with parents. When the teacher or team prepares for the conference with

Table 7.16   Student Information Sheet

Team 7-3 BATS
Student Information

The best place to begin a profile of our team of learners is to gather what is already known about each student. We can't think of a better place to start than with those who know the learner best—you. We ask you to reflect on observations you have made as your daughter or son has grown and to take a few minutes to complete this survey. Feel free to leave some sections blank if they do not apply.

Please return this survey to your child's advisory teacher. In advance, we thank you for your cooperation and the time involved in answering these questions. This information will help us develop the best learning strategies for your student.

Student's name: _____

1. Organizational skills help students succeed. Please rate your child's organizational habits (for example, strategies used to maintain her/his room or to approach a project, even a "fun" recreational project) with a rating from "1" low to "10" high.

       1   2   3   4   5   6   7   8   9   10

2. Please offer suggestions to improve your child's school organizational skills.

3. What motivates your daughter or son?

4. Which academic and/or exploratory subject is your child's strongest? Weakest?

5. What learning area (curricular subject or skill) would you like to see emphasized?

6. What social skills would you like to see your child develop?

7. Describe your child's persistence level. Include problem-solving strategies that work best for your son or daughter.

8. How difficult have you and your student found the workload to be? Too light? Too heavy?

9. What "talents" does your daughter or son have? Talents might include but are not limited to the following: music, such as piano and other instruments or singing; dance; athletics of all sorts; art; being a friend to others; being a listener; being a doer; mathematics; reading, especially materials unusual for this age and/or ability; speaking. Feel free to give examples.

10. List five words that best describe your daughter or son's character (for example, competitive, cheerful, perfectionist, procrastinator, leader, follower). For each of the words you choose, provide specific examples that help us to understand your child's individuality as an important member of your family.

specific knowledge about the student, they reinforce the trust of the parents in the team's ability to meet student needs. Further, if the team relates the positive traits of the student either prior to the meeting or at the beginning of the meeting, the possibility of parent defensiveness diminishes. During preparation, veteran teachers facilitate conference success by sharing their experience and mentoring less-experienced colleagues.

Any conference or contact with a parent requires planning and specific information. A conference data sheet completed by each member of the team guides this preparation. Often the advisory teacher assumes responsibility for this contact by presenting the data to the parent during a phone conference or when the parent comes to school for a meeting. The data, along with any agreed-upon interventions, become a part of the student's team folder, with a copy given to parents. Although Table 7.17 presents a segment of a conference data sheet, teams are encouraged to develop one that is customized for their community, school, and small learning community and focuses on the specific subjects taught.

When the team develops its planning schedule for the year, it designates a day on which parent conferences may be held. Besides determining the day, the team must be protective of its meeting time and limit most conferences to 15–20 minutes. One member of the team can be the timekeeper for the conference.

In addition to time considerations and specific information about subject area progress, the following suggestions facilitate positive conferences with parents (Merenbloom, 1991):

- Teachers reflect empathy, encouragement, and sincerity.
- Parents can see an individual teacher without meeting with the entire team.
- The conference data sheet helps to structure the discussion.
- Each teacher makes a brief statement regarding the student's performance. The statement should include positive attributes, including examples and details.
- Teachers should listen carefully to parent responses.
- Teachers should offer constructive suggestions to help a student improve.
- Team members should closely monitor the reaction of parents and be prepared to intercede when verbal and/or nonverbal cues indicate.
- Summary statements need to be confirmed by all participants.
- A follow-up plan requires the commitment of all conference participants.

Student-Led Conferences

Student-led conferences allow the student to take an active role in presenting and explaining work that is often a part of a portfolio. With increasing frequency, students use learning style or multiple-intelligence survey results to show how their work either augments their learning style or helps them to work on a weaker area. While at first artifacts may be limited to writing pieces and math papers, eventually both formative and summative assessments and other subject area projects will be included.

Table 7.17   Conference Data Sheet

Student:
Grading Period: Date: Reading Scores: Writing Assessment(s):
Course:
Teacher: Present Grade: Quality of Work: Timeliness of work: Missing work: Investment in learning (e.g., behavior, participation, politeness, time-on-task):
Comments:

According to Arnold and Stevenson (1998), student-led conferencing promotes greater accountability for learning, which is in turn realized by both student and parent. Through the student's active participation in assessing and presenting assigned work to the parent, the student simultaneously demonstrates to the teacher or team the level of understanding achieved.

Jackson and Davis (2000) relate an account of the initiation of student-led conferences in California. The participating teachers reported that involving the students eliminated the adversarial air that sometimes arises in conferences. The California teachers slowly introduced the various parts of the conference for which students would be responsible. As students became more adept, additional parts were added. During the sessions, students conducted the conference while teachers facilitated the experience (p. 201). In this type of conference, the focus is on the classroom and learning, not behavior. If behavior is an issue, traditional teacher-parent conferences may need to occur.

SUMMARY

Implementing organizational goals contributes to the mastery of the teaming process. Like the goals for the role and function of the small learning community discussed in Chapter 6, choices of organizational goals need to be reasonable in number and achievable. Without the goal-setting approach for the implementation of these elements, teachers or teams may experience a sense of being overwhelmed.

A Guide for Collaborative Conversations

To set the stage for a fuller understanding of a goal-setting process, the following questions, which focus on organizational considerations of teams or small learning communities, serve as a guide to achieving a direct impact on curriculum and instruction.

Leader Questions

1. How will the school/district establish the spectrum of organizational goals?

2. How will teachers begin to see the relationship between goals for organization and goals for curriculum and instruction?

3. What process will be used to enable cohorts of teachers to inventory their strengths and limitations in relationship to the goals in the organizational category?

4. What staff development resources will be available to help teachers achieve goals identified in this chapter?

5. How will the total goal-setting process be evaluated?

Teacher Questions

1. What criteria should be used to select organizational goals?

2. On a yearly basis, how should the number of goals from Chapter 7 be determined?

3. What resources will be available as we pursue our goals?

4. How will the total goal-setting process be evaluated?

8

Teaching in Variable-Length Time Periods

Successful schools and small learning communities recognize that the enhancement of student learning must be the goal of any schedule or restructuring process. Consequently, their effective use of a master schedule and implementation of the role and function of a team require professional inquiry into an adaptation of creative teaching strategies. Simply changing the schedule or forming teams will not produce the desired learning experiences for students (Arhar, Johnston, & Markle, 1992b; NASSP, 1996).

Ideally, schedules have the capability to provide extended time periods on a fixed or variable basis. Either fixed or variable use of extended time periods can advance the desirable combination of essential learning and adequate time for learning. Fixed periods of extended time occur in day 1/day 2 and semester 1/ semester 2 schedules. In these schedules, all classes meet for extended periods each day of the school year. Opportunities for variable periods of extended time exist in interdisciplinary team-maximum flexibility, combination team, and rotational schedules. Although these schedules contain periods of 40–50 minutes, variable length modules can be created. Utilizing control over time afforded by these schedules, teachers opt for 45-minute classes, 60- to 90-minute classes, or some other combination, depending on the needs of students and the focus of the small learning community.

Within this chapter, suggestions appear for teaching in variable time periods. Models of research-based ideas and strategies enable the planning of instruction, including the identification of the essential learning necessary for the subject or unit taught. Within fixed or variable structures, the following planning models enable teachers to develop variable-length lessons: pacing guide, unit development plan, and lesson plan prototype. As stated previously, the ultimate objective of reorganization is to increase student achievement.

PACING GUIDE

Textbook content and the standards movement contribute to the overwhelming amount of curriculum to be taught. Both Erickson (2001) and Marzano (2003) caution against the attempt to cover all possible topics and facts. They encourage the distillation of the possible content into essential learnings. Erickson suggests that without a focus on "deeper, transferable understandings," instruction becomes a form of "trivial pursuit" (p. 20). Her presentation of concept-based instruction includes the work of Heidi Hayes-Jacobs in curriculum mapping as a way to identify the district's intended curriculum.

From the map of the intended curriculum, teachers identify the essential learnings as well as the K–12 alignment of content and skills (Hayes-Jacobs, 1997). The map implies the structure or sequence of instruction for the year. Similarly, Marzano (2003) recommends the identification of essential declarative and procedural knowledge. Declarative knowledge refers to information presented and learned while procedural knowledge refers to skill or process (p. 114). Identified essential learnings form the basis of a rigorous curriculum and the focus of formative and summative assessment (NASSP, 2006). Once identified, the content should be sequenced so that adequate time exists for students to have the necessary opportunity to learn.

As teachers prepare to teach in extended time periods on a fixed or variable basis, they transfer the essential or target learnings from the curriculum map and set them in a pacing guide. By plotting the essential learning and allocating time to support the opportunity to learn, teachers are more able to ensure that the essential intended curriculum will be covered by the end of the course. According to Hayes-Jacobs (1997), if a commitment does not exist for when something will be taught, it will not be taught (p. 4). The pacing guide lists units of instruction with start and completion dates for each unit. Table 8.1 illustrates a middle school pacing guide for the chronological presentation of American history.

When schools or districts develop horizontal and vertical articulation of curriculum and promote consistency in instruction, pacing guides should be a collaborative effort by all teachers in a building or district who teach the same subject. The pacing guide becomes the basis of long-term planning for the course and long-term planning for the magnet, house, academy, or small learning community. Within the timeframe presented in the pacing guide, teachers integrate curriculum by applying other instructional elements contained in the curriculum map. In interdisciplinary–maximum flexibility, combination team, or rotational schedules, teachers can plan for either 45-minute or extended periods; however, the start and completion dates of units must be seen as fixed.

Table 8.1 Pacing Guide

Course:	American History: Part I
Grade Level:	7
Structural Option(s):	Interdisciplinary–Maximum Flexibility or Rotational

Weeks	Units of Instruction	Start Date	Completion Date
1	Introduction to Study Skills and Procedures	August 23	August 30
3	Exploration and Cultures	August 31	September 21
3	Colonization and Beginning of Governmental Structures	September 22	October 13
4	Steps Toward Independence	October 14	November 11
3	Establishing Independence	November 12	December 1
6	The Structure of Government	December 2	January 24
3	The Imprint of Government Philosophies	January 25	February 15
3	Industrialization	February 16	March 9
3	Becoming Self-Sufficient: The Dialogues	March 31	April 28
3	Civil War: Defining State and Federal Domains	April 29	May 20
4	Reconstruction	May 23	June 13
36 weeks			

UNIT DEVELOPMENT PLAN

Units listed in the pacing guide must be expanded into specific content, skills, and applications to real life situations. As discussed earlier, Erickson (2001) and Marzano (2003) caution against the focus on facts alone, reminding educators that content is just a vehicle for encouraging deeper thought. Wiggins and McTighe (1998), as well, explain the danger of emphasizing facts rather than understanding. They recall a story of John Dewey's in which he asked questions of a class regarding the structure of the earth. Students were not able to answer his questions until he asked the question in the exact format in which the students learned the content (p. 39). Students had not learned how to transfer the information to a broader context.

The authors of *Breaking Ranks* (NASSP, 1996) note that without depth of instruction and connections between subjects, knowledge is distorted (p. 13). Besides the addition of content, skills, and applications, previously chosen goals and subject area standards are applied and integrated into instructional delivery. By working together with other subject area specialists, the curriculum becomes more consistent and articulated.

One format that not only meets the needs of students but incorporates essential learning and opportunities for deep thinking comes from the work of

Dr. William Alexander. He believed that curriculum exists in three parts: organized knowledge or key content, skill development, and personal development or applications to real-life situations (George & Alexander, 1993). His format corresponds with Marzano's recommendations to include declarative and procedural knowledge in instruction. In an impassioned support of curriculum integration, Gordon Vars (1969, cited in Vars, 2001, p. 11) reinforces the need to integrate "life skills" into curriculum design. He reminds educators that some goals of education move beyond subject area content and into areas that promote "effective functioning as a citizen and human being."

Supporting the implementation of teaching in variable time periods and the Alexander curriculum format, Bransford and colleagues (2000), in their publication, *How People Learn,* reinforce the importance of structuring the delivery of instruction with an adequate time factor embedded for understanding. In order to achieve understanding but also to focus on the motivational aspects of learning, they connect the social and practical implications of learning with student motivation and engagement.

Bransford et al. (2000) further indicate that instruction needs to vary, addressing both performance-oriented and learning-oriented student needs. Performance-oriented students struggle with overconcern about making errors; learning-oriented students relish new challenges (Dweck, 1989, cited in Bransford et al., 2000, p. 61). Consequently, differentiation strategies need to be incorporated into the plan of the unit.

Similarly, Pat Wolfe (2001) stresses the importance of the relevance of curriculum. She presents three questions to be asked prior to curriculum development: "'What are the big ideas or concepts?,' 'What is the life-long benefit of what I'm teaching?,' and 'How will students be able to use what they are learning today in their adult lives?'" (p. 132). Her questions parallel Alexander's component parts of a curriculum: key content, life-long skills, and real-life application. To illustrate the model, a format for the unit development plan appears in Table 8.2 and a specific example is provided in Table 8.3.

Table 8.2   Unit Development Plan Model

Course:

Conceptual Lens:

Grade Level:

Unit:

Main Thrust:

   A. Key Content

   B. Skills

   C. Applications to Real-Life Situations

Essential Questions:

Table 8.3 Unit Development Plan Example

Course: American History: Part I

Conceptual Lens: Relationships

Grade Level: 7

Unit: Steps Toward Independence

Main Thrust: Freedom requires the just and equal application of the law.

A. Key Content
   1. Background ideas from history that influenced English Colonial ideas about government
   2. English Acts and actions that provoked responses from colonists
   3. Concepts and ideas in the Declaration of Independence: Just and equal?

B. Skills
   1. Identification of main ideas
   2. Compare and contrast
   3. Cause and effect
   4. Inferences
   5. Prediction
   6. Evaluation

C. Applications to Real-Life Situations
   1. Understanding that ideas, discoveries, or inventions are often a result of ideas that have come before
   2. Collaborative work sets the stage for the development or synthesis of new ideas
   3. Relationships can be positive, negative, or neutral

Essential Questions

A. In what ways did aspects of earlier English history and the colonists' own history influence their ideas about freedom?
B. How did English law affect the thinking and actions of the colonists?
C. Why did English law become the predominant factor in developing a New World government rather than Spanish or French law?

Through the completion of the unit development plan, teachers are better able to see the integration and strategy needs of the unit. The identification of essential questions allows teachers to proceed in developing comprehensive daily lesson plans that incorporate targeted content, skills, and authentic applications. During the course of the unit, planned instruction prepares students to answer the questions with extended responses.

LESSON PLAN PROTOTYPE

Using information gleaned from the unit development plan, teachers plan daily lessons based on the model in Table 8.4.

Table 8.4   Lesson Plan Prototype Segment

CONCEPTUAL LENS _____

UNIT TITLE _____

Session Number _____   Number of Sessions in Unit _____

MAIN THRUST:
ESSENTIAL QUESTION(S):
LEARNING ENGAGEMENT #1   Topic _____   Time _____
Purpose:
Motivation:
Recall:
Engagement:
Assessment:
Connection:

LEARNING ENGAGEMENT #2   Topic _____   Time _____
Purpose:
Motivation:
Recall:
Engagement:
Assessment:
Connection:

LEARNING ENGAGEMENT #3   Topic _____   Time _____
Purpose:
Motivation:
Recall:
Engagement:
Assessment:
Connection:

Additional learning engagements are added to fit the length of the class period.

Initially, teachers determine the main thrust or goals of each lesson. Marzano (2003) stresses the importance of clear goals in order to develop a functional instructional framework (p. 85). He notes that teachers who establish clear learning goals for students enable them to perform at higher achievement levels. Stiggins (2001) concurs by stating that students can hit any target that is clearly identified and explained. Expanding upon Marzano's statistics illustrating expected performance goals (pp. 36–37), teachers share main thrusts or key understandings within a unit by scaffolding engagements toward those achievement levels.

Wiggins and McTighe (1998) call the main thrust or goal the "enduring understanding" to be sought in instruction—that is, the understanding that students will retain and be able to transfer. Their criteria for selecting an enduring understanding include determining the value of the idea beyond the classroom, the importance of the idea to the particular discipline, the depth of the idea, and the potential of the idea for engaging students (pp. 10–11). Erickson's (2001) reference to "generalizations" implies a main thrust that is the synthesis of two or more elements from the unit design (p. 84).

Main Thrust, Essential Questions, Conceptual Lens

Working with the major ideas or constructs within the unit plan, the main thrust of a given lesson includes key content, skills, and/or applications to life. Although the main thrust guides the teacher in planning, it needs to be shared with the students verbally and through posting in the room (Erickson, 2001; Hayes-Jacobs, 1997; Wiggins & McTighe, 1998). By sharing the intent of instruction with students, the teacher provides a clear target to identify the learning upon which assessment will be based (Stiggins, 2001).

For students to arrive at an understanding of a main thrust, they need guides. The most engaging guides exist in the form of essential or guide questions (Erickson, 2001; Wiggins & McTighe, 1998). Wiggins and McTighe suggest the use of questions that take the learner beyond surface learning: "provocative and multilayered" to "reveal the richness and complexities of the subject" (p. 28). Erickson (2001) encourages questions that move the student toward a conceptual understanding. "What" questions keep the student's thinking process at the factual level; "why" and "how" questions provide avenues for deeper thought (p. 92). The design of the questions takes the student into the content and central ideas of the subject area. Like the main thrust, the questions need to be shared with students, posted in the room, and connected to the instruction and assessment process repeatedly during the lesson and the unit. Probing for answers to essential questions produces intrinsic realization of the main thrust stated in the students' own words.

Along with the broad design of the major essential questions, teachers may find it helpful to construct more specific questions that relate to the unit or specific content being studied. These questions provide a more concrete learning scaffold for the student and an additional basis for engagements that comprise the lesson. To promote more inquiry on the part of students, neither form of question should be answered in a word or single sentence. Not only do both forms of question purposefully "frame the learning [and] engage the learner" (Wiggins & McTighe, 1998, p. 30), but they provide the basis for formative and summative assessment. Ultimately, the learning and understanding gained from focusing instruction on the main thrust and promoting inquiry into the essential questions provide the student with the ability to achieve success in the assessment process.

In the model lesson plan, both the main thrust and the essential questions contribute to an understanding of the lesson's concept focus. Erickson (2001) defines concept or "conceptual lens" as the integrating idea for a unit. The use of concept as a broad idea, timeless and abstract, promotes transfer between disciplines. As modeled in Table 8.5, the concept can be presented by a single word.

Table 8.5   Conceptual Lens Terminology

Mathematics:	systems, patterns, interrelationships, cycle, order
Science:	change, pattern, cycle, category, power, force, order
Social Studies:	change, conflict, cycle, systems, power, forces, adaptation
Art:	pattern, system, relationship, change, power, order
English:	relationship, pattern, order
Music:	pattern, order, cycle

McTighe and Wiggins (1998) cite Bruner (1960), who determined that the understanding of a subject lay in understanding the underlying principles of the subject (p. 72). Likewise, Tomlinson refers to Hilda Taba's work by describing the importance of concept as a unifying factor of learning. Through the commonalities of a given concept, the integration of understanding and knowledge takes place (Tomlinson, 1999, p. 38). The broad concept allows thinking to move to a larger level of transfer.

Bransford et al. (2000) reason that if experts organize their knowledge around concepts, curriculum should be organized in similar fashion (p. 42). Their thinking is echoed in the work of others who encourage teachers to make experts from novices by helping students develop patterns in the information presented (Erickson, 2001; Sousa, 2006; Tomlinson, 1999).

Learning Engagements

The foundation for student success rests on a series of carefully constructed activities, scaffolds, or learning engagements that lead to formative or summative assessment. The essential question(s) and main thrust of the unit or lesson form the basis for these assessments and guide the sequence of the learning engagements. Together, the elements present the clear target Stiggins (2001) advocates when teachers assess for learning.

In *Turning Points 2000*, Jackson and Davis (2000) caution against developing "showy" culminating tasks for the "cool" factor. They describe Coila Morrow's disdain of the "hands-on" types of activities that do not relate to the standards or concept focus of the unit or lesson. Morrow bemoans the pervasiveness of learning Texas history through building sugar cube Alamos (cited in Jackson & Davis, pp. 51–52) and Pat Wolfe (2001) cautions in the same vein that students need to see the purpose of the activities and the connection to clearly targeted learning: "Projects and activities should be a means to enhance learning, not an end in themselves" (p. 142). Throughout the lesson, active engagements should enable the student to answer one or more open-ended questions that reflect student mastery of goals established through the synergy between main thrust and essential questions. Besides adding to the student's store of knowledge, engagements enable students to see patterns and relationships.

Ideally, learning engagements provide a scaffold, moving the students from the introduction to the day's lesson to a culminating understanding. This format reflects David Sousa's (2006) examination of factors influencing retention. In his discussion, Sousa focuses on the primacy-recency effect in retention and the resulting influence of prime-time and down-time in the class period. The primacy-recency effect refers to the time in a class period when learning takes place: The most powerful learning time occurs at the beginning of the session; the second most powerful occurs at the end. Because information presented during these prime times will most likely be remembered, teachers need to take care that only correct information is presented or reinforced. In the down-time that follows prime learning time, developmental or reinforcing engagements take place. These engagements give the learner processing time, including opportunities for review or other forms of reflective engagements (pp. 88–89).

Sousa (2006) further identifies the importance of time when delivering instruction. He notes that 20-minute segments create less down-time than longer learning segments. Consequently, planning several short activities for a class period ensures more prime-time learning and decreases the amount of down-time, as seen in Tables 8.6 and 8.7. Additionally, by planning several shorter segments within a class period, the teacher includes novelty, an element that gains the attention of the brain and fits the quick-paced lives of most students. This format can be implemented in 40-minute classes or extended time (pp. 91–92).

Table 8.6   Prime-Time and Down-Time in Learning Episodes

	Prime-Times		Down-Time	
Episode Time	Total Number of Minutes	Percentage of Total Time	Number of Minutes	Percentage of Total time
20 minutes	18	90	2	10
40 minutes	30	75	10	25
80 minutes	50	62	30	38

SOURCE: Sousa, D. A. (2006). *How the brain learns* (3rd ed.). Thousand Oaks, CA: Corwin Press.

While the study of memory impacts Sousa's connection of learning to time and sequencing, cognitive psychology structures Marzano's (2003) three principles of learning: (1) identifying the learning goals, communicating them to students, and designing instruction around them; (2) engaging students in structured tasks that allow transfer; and (3) providing opportunities for repetition and interaction with knowledge (pp. 108–112). As advice to accomplish these principles, he urges teachers to make decisions on the sequencing and pacing of instruction rather than relying on textbook sequencing.

The observations of Sousa and Marzano reinforce the structure of the lesson plan modeled in this chapter. This plan features a conceptual lens realized through the main thrust, content delivered through a series of connected learning engagements, and assessed via the essential questions.

Table 8.7   Average Prime- and Down-Times in Learning Engagements: Minutes and Percentages of Time

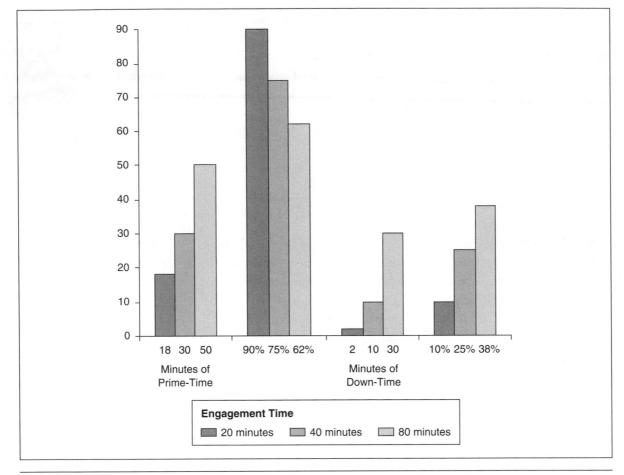

SOURCE: Sousa, D.A. (2006). *How the brain learns* (3rd ed.). Thousand Oaks, CA: Corwin Press.

The learning engagements provide students with opportunities to master the complexities of the conceptual aspect or main thrust of a lesson. One opportunity involves "chunking" material into small units to be stored as a single item in long-term memory. Within these chunked units, students find patterns that allow more efficient storage of knowledge. Later, during a problem-solving engagement, the chunked information can be recalled more efficiently into working memory.

Noting that chunking is not an innate ability, Sousa (2006) identifies two forms of chunking that can be taught: pattern and categorical (pp. 129–130). Pattern chunking occurs in the use of numbers, words, and repetitive procedures; categorical chunking requires the learner to categorize the information, much like Marzano's (2003) instructional strategy category of identifying similarities and differences.

In concurrence with that instructional strategy, Marzano (2003) suggests grouping material around the importance of "sameness" within the content. Citing James Flavell (1971), Marzano equates sameness grouping with the structure needed to enhance learning (pp. 111–112). Each of these theories supports the need for student engagement to help students inductively reach the desired conclusion(s) and answer the essential question(s).

Student engagements that promote understanding come from the material to be learned and the motivation of students. In designing the engagements for a particular lesson, teachers need to recall Sousa's (2006) examples of the importance of short learning episodes to heighten retention, connection, and, ultimately, understanding. Additionally, the engagements need to change in type and pace. For example, an individual segment such as a writing reflection follows a group discussion activity (Marzano, 2003, p. 116).

Williams and Dunn (2000) cite the study of Ron Fitzgerald (1996) that focuses on the importance of mixing activities with high degrees of intensity with activities that allow for reflection and processing. Sousa identifies the basis for this fluctuating need: working memory can handle only a few items at once. Therefore, a shift in the activity is needed in order to maintain interest or engagement. If a change in the activity does not take place, the possibility lessens for the information to move into long-term memory (pp. 45–46).

While planning learning engagements, teachers need to consider the learners' abilities to move from concrete to abstract ideas. Brain research experts remind curriculum developers to provide concrete experiences as prior learning for representational and abstract learning. Without concrete understanding, no amount of explanation will make a representation or symbol meaningful. Additionally, abstract ideas such as "democracy" and mathematics concepts require purposeful connections to students' prior experiences and active involvement in scaffolding designed to make the abstraction understandable.

Problem solving that relates to real life forms one of the strongest accommodations to learning through experiences (Wolfe, 2001). These experiences are enhanced when connected by episodic memory, the form of memory prompted by location and circumstance. These memories, however, can contaminate learning when the experiences deprive the learner of novelty. The contamination can be minimized through a change of seating, rooms, or presentation forms (Jensen, 1998b).

Marzano (2003) also implies that sequencing forms of instruction impacts student learning. His research indicates that students learn best when introduced to a new concept through some form of dramatization followed by discussion and finally argumentation or a defense of the conclusions regarding the instruction. Similarly, Sylwester (1995) maintains that dramatization reinforces long-term memory.

Although Marzano emphasizes the importance of structuring instruction apart from the textbook, he cautions against the misuse of constructivist instruction or instruction based solely on the findings in brain research. He does, however, promote the cognitive psychologists' findings of the two forms of knowledge, declarative and procedural, discussed earlier in this chapter. As noted by those leaders in the field of brain research, Marzano, too, recommends practice to reach the desired levels of learning and understanding (pp. 113–114). In brain research this process is termed *rehearsal* (Jensen, 1998a; Sousa, 2006; Sylwester, 1995; Wolfe, 2001). The lesson plan prototype presents opportunities for practice and rehearsal within the series of learning engagements.

Considerable research supports moving learners through a series of connected experiences. To support teachers in this paradigm shift, instructional leaders provide staff development in the context of specific curriculum areas. This support enables the teacher to master the art of designing these engagements.

Learning Engagement Strategies

A variety of instructional strategies should be used to constitute a series of learning engagements: group work, cooperative learning, learning stations, simulations, dramatizations, skits, guided reading activities, graphic organizers, projects, use of technology, and note-taking opportunities.

Group work and *cooperative learning* meet students' personal development and social needs, while providing an avenue for mutual success. More highly structured than group work, cooperative learning groups employ specific roles to be performed by individual students. Both forms require teacher guidance in the areas of rules and behaviors to enhance the learning environment. Both include a form of reflection and processing of accomplishments during the assigned task.

Kagan (1994) refers to cooperative learning as a series of structures in which the content can be infused. By changing either the structure or the content, the learning engagement or activity takes on a different focus, allowing teachers to differentiate instruction. According to Wheelock, a variety of studies indicate that students will persevere longer on a problem when working with a group than when working alone (1998). Care needs to be taken, however, not to use group or cooperative learning excessively. When alternated with more individual formats, group work maintains interest and reinforces multiple ways of learning.

To provide students with active engagement opportunities, *learning stations* allow additional differentiation formats. Designed for individual, cooperative, or differentiated formats, thematically developed stations allow students to move at their own pace (Schurr, Lewis, LaMorte, & Shewey, 1996). In planning the stations, teachers begin with their curriculum map and unit development plan. They follow with the design for learning engagements in the model lesson plan. The resulting criteria, posted at each station, provide a basis for student self-assessment.

Simulations, demonstrations, and skits are some of the *dramatization* forms encouraged by Marzano (2003) and others for prime retention and learning. Dramatizations, too, need to have guidelines, fit the main thrust, and lead the learner to an understanding of the essential questions.

Guided reading applies to all content areas. Various professional organizations and literacy experts note the lack of these skills in secondary students. Spurred by the increasingly complex demands of the twenty-first century, five organizations collaborated on a document intended to coach secondary teachers in the teaching of content area reading and writing: the National Council of Teachers of English, the National Council of Teachers of Mathematics, the National Council for the Social Studies, the National Science Teachers Association, and the International Reading Association (2005). Their sense of urgency arises from the fact that few content area teachers are trained to implement literacy strategies. The research by the organizations caused them to recognize that one in four adolescents cannot identify the main idea in a passage. These problems are especially pronounced in reading textbooks, technical reading, and other forms of nonfiction.

While some strategies lend themselves to middle/junior high school instruction, most cross into the high school arena. Some strategies encourage metacognition as well as model individual interaction with the text: "Think Aloud" and Directed Reading Thinking Activity (DRTA). Others aid students in group work to uncover meaning: know-want to know-learned (K-W-L) forms and "Say Something" activities. Vocabulary study becomes embedded in content area instruction rather than a fragmented subject relegated to the language arts class (Allen, 2004; Beers, 2003; Biancarosa & Snow, 2004; Faber, 2004; NCTE et al., 2005). The use of guided reading activities promotes reflection and gives learners time to make connections between what they know, what has been presented, and how it can be further applied. By threading these strategies across the subject areas, teams or small learning communities provide the needed repetition for building automaticity of skills and integration of instruction.

Graphic organizers such as timelines, fishbones, and word webs provide the impact of visual connection to the focused learning. They allow learners to see patterns of organized information: descriptive for facts, time-sequence for chronology, cause-and-effect for causal effects, episodic for specific events, and conceptual for organized concepts with attributes and examples (Marzano, Pickering, & Pollock, 2001). The visual effect provides a pathway to representational learning that reinforces the main thrust. As advance organizers, they provide the bridge between what the student knows and what is to be learned.

Projects need to be thoughtfully developed and assigned. As noted earlier, projects must have a direct connection to the conceptual lens, main thrust, or essential questions that form the basis of the learning. Further, the time required to complete a project should be in line with its importance to the learning and the importance of the lesson to the overall unit. If the project requires work at home, guidelines for parent involvement must be clearly communicated, emphasizing the importance of facilitation over direct involvement (Marzano et al., 2001). In some cases, the project may be better completed over a period of days during a designated part of the lesson, allowing teachers to give the student formative feedback and individual responsibility. This format works well with problem-based learning, projects that require the development and testing of a hypothesis, or the development of a piece of writing.

The immersion of *technology* into the classroom takes judicious planning and guidance. If students have been taught keyboarding, they will write more quickly and fluently than when writing in cursive. When using developed keyboarding skills, students use typing speeds that correlate with thinking speeds (Sylwester, 1995). Consequently, revision becomes more acceptable to the student who does not have to rewrite the piece several times in cursive.

The world of the Internet opens vast reservoirs of information to students and allows them to establish new forms of communication through Web sites. Moreover, it reflects the world of work today rather than the Industrial Age concept of school (Senge et al., 2000). Like other instructional strategies, however, the use of technology requires prudent oversight. For instance, when students prepare reports or presentations, they need to focus on the main thrust of the engagement rather than merely play with the colorful effects of a program or surf the Internet.

Exposure to interactive programs often provides both focus and feedback. Newer technologies contain a vast array of information, visual graphing capabilities, and problem-based simulation activities, providing the student with higher level and more complex thinking opportunities. Additional technology opportunities include video and electronic communication systems. Students interact with experts through a variety of these systems. Active engagement in programming robots or designing pieces of architecture or landscaping incorporates problem-solving techniques.

As with other instructional strategies, the application of all technology requires a coherent connection to the conceptual lens, main thrust, and essential questions of the lesson or unit. With those goals in mind, the thoughtful incorporation of technology into the lesson plan can fulfill all three of Alexander's curriculum modes: content, skills, and real-life application.

Note taking teaches the student to isolate the big ideas of a text, discussion, or lecture. Research on note taking indicates that students should not attempt to record all of the information presented, that notes are a work in progress, and that notes offer excellent test preparation (Beecher, 1988, cited in Marzano et al., 2001). It is, however, a skill that must be taught and appears in a variety of forms.

One type of note taking exists in several names and formats: combination notes, T-notes, and double-entry data (DED) notes. Each of these formats uses a vertical line that divides the page into two parts. Combination notes place information in an informal outline structure on the left; visualizations of the information on the right; and, in a space at the bottom, a summary statement of the information (Marzano et al., 2001). T-notes and DED notes place significant, critical, or big ideas on the left with details on the right. These forms can be expanded to three columns such as those used in a K-W-L activity (Ogle, 1986, cited in Allen, 2004; Faber, 2004).

The TED or triple-entry data notes encourage students to think beyond the text or lecture and develop applications or questions of their own regarding the material presented. Metacognitive points written in the third column are intended to provoke discussion or further investigation. Tomlinson suggests this format as a method of differentiation (1999). When small learning communities, teams, departments, grade levels, or schools use the same format, the process becomes automatic for the student who can easily transfer the skill to other arenas as well as use it as a format for keeping vocabulary and other lists requiring memorization.

Today's student population comes from an increasingly diverse society that presents challenges to and expectations of the teacher. Therefore, when deciding the strategies to be used in the lesson plan, thought should be given to what Tomlinson (1999) calls a "learning profile" (p. 14) similar to the profiles based on developmental needs found in Chapter 5. With this information, teachers can develop various forms of differentiation to meet students' intelligences, learning modalities, and other elements of that learning profile. When front-loaded in the planning or goal-setting stages, each of these components becomes easier to incorporate.

Differentiation occurs in classrooms in which teachers begin at the level of students' understanding. The teacher considers the content, process, and product of each lesson and adapts it to meet student needs and to ensure student success (Tomlinson, 1999). Therefore, the establishment of a conceptual lens, main thrust, and the essential questions becomes a necessity for instructional consistency. These elements of the lesson plan prototype offer a bridge for differentiation.

Formative and summative assessments conducted throughout the lesson reveal each student's level of understanding of the conceptual lens, main thrust, or the essential questions and provide the teacher with guidelines for pacing. One differentiation method, circle-seat-center, reaches various ability levels of students and provides formative assessment information. Students having difficulty with a specific task meet in a circle with the teacher for re-teaching; students understanding the task but needing practice work independently in their seats; students demonstrating a keen understanding of the task work at a learning center created for those who can pursue a more complex uncovering of the lesson.

Through the use of varied methods and levels of instruction, teachers facilitate student progress toward goals of instruction. A part of that facilitation occurs through satisfying the brain's need for movement and novelty, both differentiation processes. Another part involves *formative assessments* the inclusion of smaller pieces of assessment and feedback that guide instruction toward identified essential learnings. *Summative assessment*, too, varies in formats that allow students to demonstrate their understanding. Instead of total reliance on pencil and paper end-of-unit tests, students develop presentations, devise projects, or maintain a portfolio that integrates the desired essential learning.

Two additional ways in which differentiation can occur include *learning styles* and *modalities*. Although meeting a student's learning style or differentiating instruction does not refer to the individualized instruction of an earlier time in the history of education, it does require understanding that each brain learns differently. The way in which prior learning and new information mesh within the brain is unique for each student (Jensen, 1998b).

The work of Howard Gardner as cited in Campbell, Campbell, & Dickinson (1996) reveals various forms of intelligence that impact learning. Multiple resources exist on these theories to give teachers substantive background for incorporating effective ways to engage each of the forms. Learning stations and learning style assessments create an opportunity to address students' natural ways of learning. Caution needs to be taken so that lessons are not stretched artificially to include multiple identified intelligences in one lesson or series of learning engagements. The strategies that fit this form of instruction, like all others, must fit the content.

Consequently, the challenge to the teacher lies in the ability to identify and categorize students' learning styles. Each student's needs are eventually met within the design of the overall lesson without creating individual lessons for each student or consistently using large group instruction. Besides focusing on the student's strengths, the lesson design can recognize the student's weaker areas so that a level of strength in those areas may develop. Additionally, a knowledge of students' learning styles benefits the grouping and regrouping process so that variety is achieved and constant homogeneity is avoided.

Throughout the design of learning engagements, the pacing guide, unit development plan, and the lesson plan prototype should be continuously monitored for possible additions and adaptations. In keeping with the theories concerning brain research, cognitive psychology, differentiation, and learning styles, the learning engagement process features a variety of ways to create connections that lead the student to an understanding of the lesson's essential questions, the unit's main thrust, and, ultimately, the conceptual lens. In part, the student's attention span limitations guide the number of engagements included on a given day. When following the lesson plan prototype, teachers can successfully lead students to an inductive understanding of these learning goals.

LEARNING ENGAGEMENT DESIGN

The lesson plan prototype in Table 8.4 provides an opportunity for teachers of all subjects to plan effectively for extended time periods. The plan reflects research reviewed in this chapter and serves as a means to implement the research to improve student learning. Depending on the lesson, four to six engagements are developed, including opening and closing engagements.

When designing learning engagements, several facets need to be considered: time, intended curriculum, varied strategies, assessments, and connections. Time includes various elements. One element, the primacy-recency effect, encourages better comprehension and memory of the material. Although the primacy-recency effect generally refers to the prime-time-1, or beginning, and prime-time-2, or end, of the lesson time frame, it contributes to the retention gained when lessons are divided into 10- to 20-minute segments (see Tables 8.6 and 8.7). The novelty of each new learning engagement gives the learner a new primacy-recency time period and reduces down-time.

Since the brain cannot stay focused at an intense level for an extended period, effective learning engagements require a change in pace and focus: an active or interactive segment followed by a connecting reflective segment. Physical activity incorporated into some of the segments or as a part of the down-time engagements energizes the learner and relieves some of the intensity of the lesson (Jensen, 1998b). If a period of direct instruction or lecturing is required, Sousa suggests it occur at the beginning of the lesson and appear only once in the duration of the lesson (2006).

Time further impacts the opportunity to learn the intended curriculum. The curriculum is dictated in part by district, state, and national standards but can be unpacked to reveal the essential learning and chunked so that learners have time to process the concepts taught. By isolating the essential learning, teachers pace the instruction, practice, and assessment to meet the needs of all students through differentiation. Some learners can be introduced to more complex versions of a concept while others may need additional practice to understand the essential learning.

To promote continuity of instruction, strategies should be discussed and shared by members of the small learning community, department, or grade level. Threading similar strategies through different subject areas allows the student to rehearse either a skill or a concept. It is imperative to note that when introducing new concepts and material, concrete or prior learning engagements should be an integral part of sequencing lessons.

An understanding of the time of day optimal for learning contributes to the choice of learning engagements and assessments. High school students' attention rhythms occur later in the day than elementary students. For example, testing later in the morning or in the early afternoon benefits the high school student but not the elementary student (Sousa, 2006). Unfortunately, assessment cannot always meet this criterion because schedules are often fixed.

The availability of variable-length time periods encourages the use of more formative and performance assessments. Formative assessment, the ongoing and often informal evaluation of student understanding, provides an opportunity for timely and pertinent feedback, which is considered to be a major factor that promotes achievement (Hattie, 1992, cited in Marzano, 2003, p. 37). It requires little more than a walk around the classroom or joining learners in a small group discussion, during which both accountability and the student level of understanding can be determined. Through a closer observation of a student's learning, understanding of the concept, and ability to respond to the essential questions, the teacher eliminates sole reliance on a summative assessment to determine student achievement and success (Falk, 2002; Felner et al., 1997; Marzano, 2003).

Referring to the lesson plan prototype segment in Table 8.4, teachers begin to focus on the design of specific learning engagements. The framework of the conceptual lens, unit title, main thrust, and essential question(s) appears in Table 8.8 and provides a guide for completion of that portion of the lesson plan. To aid in understanding the overall and specific elements of the design, guide questions follow each table.

The following guide questions are provided to promote discussion and understanding of the conceptual lens, unit title, main thrust, and essential questions:

1. How will teachers identify the conceptual lens for a lesson?

2. How will teachers identify the unit title for a lesson?

3. Within a unit of instruction, how will teachers connect the main thrust to the learning engagements?

4. How can teachers establish a relationship between learning engagements and the essential question(s)?

Table 8.9 provides a format for one specific learning engagement; Table 8.10 models six engagements that may be presented in one extended time period with an emphasis on the sequencing of those engagements. A learning engagement comprises six components: purpose, motivation, recall, student engagement, assessment, and connection. Typically, a lesson will include four to six engagements to scaffold concept development.

The guide questions that follow are provided to establish understanding of the six components of a learning engagement (purpose, motivation, recall, student engagement, assessment, and connection).

Table 8.8   Conceptual Lens, Unit Title, Main Thrust, and Essential Questions for American History Part 1, Grade 7

Component	Example	Explanation/Rationale
Conceptual Lens	Relationships: • Relationships can be positive or negative. • Relationships can bring about change. • Relationships can be natural, forced, or chosen. • Relationships can be temporary or lasting. Note: Other examples of conceptual lens topics appear in Table 8.5.	• The integrating idea for a unit; the underlying principle; the unifying factor of learning (Bruner, 1960, cited by McTighe & Wiggins, 1998; Erickson, 2001; Tomlinson, 1999) • A broad concept allowing thinking to transfer • A basis for "chunking" information or identifying "sameness" (Marzano, 2003) • Theme for an interdisciplinary unit of a small learning community
Unit Title	Steps Toward Independence	• Derived from pacing guide, curriculum map • Reflects state and national standards • May be broad in application
Main Thrust	Freedom requires the just and equal application of law.	• Broadly includes content, skills, and real-life applications • The "enduring understandings" (Wiggins & McTighe, 1998) • The understanding that the student will retain and transfer within and beyond the classroom • A clear learning goal that moves beyond facts to a broader understanding of an idea • Chosen by its relevance to the content, transferability, engagement of students' interest, depth (Wiggins & McTighe, 1998)
Essential Questions	In what ways did aspects of earlier English history and the colonists' own history influence their ideas about freedom?	• Present guides toward understanding the main thrust and concept • Take learner beyond surface learning • Use "why" and "how" questions rather than "what" • Cannot be answered in a word or sentence • Provide basis for formative and summative assessment • Serve as culminating effort of lesson and/or unit • Require chunking by teachers

**Table 8.9   Format for a Learning Engagement for American
History Part 1, Grade 7**

Component	Example	Explanation/Rationale
Purpose	To see how ideas are influenced by and build upon earlier ideas	• Establishes reasoning for the engagement • Connects to main thrust, essential questions, content, skills, or real-life applications • Reveals clear learning goals • Responds to students' questions regarding the "why" of the lesson
Motivation	Overhead image of a skateboard or an actual skateboard	• Aids students to acquire interest • Uses advance organizer strategies • Assists students in seeing connections, patterns, and relationships • Serves as anticipatory set • Connects to prior knowledge or real-life experiences
Recall	Why do we work in groups? How are groups an integral part of discussions or cooperative learning experiences?	• Establishes connections between what is known and what is to be learned • Encourages rehearsal • Occurs in horizontal form (connection to another course) or vertical form (connection to previous study) • Appears as questioning, cues, visuals, and other appropriate "connecting" strategies • Helps students retrieve skill or knowledge from long-term memory
Engagement	In small groups, list ideas/objects/toys/machines/past events that may have influenced the invention or development of the skateboard.	• Exists as a series of learner experiences that promote understanding of main thrust • Leads to successful completion of assessments • Provides a scaffold on which students build understanding: strategies, processes, experiences provided for the learner • Incorporates a variety of research-based strategies • Addresses the importance of time, rehearsal, connections, and involvement of students • Requires active participation to be beneficial

(Continued)

Table 8.9   (Continued)

Component	Example	Explanation/Rationale
Assessment	One person will report each group's responses. Teacher will list responses on board or newsprint. Class will indicate (by hand vote) which responses most likely influenced the invention of the skateboard.	• Process used to determine students' levels of understanding and readiness to move forward • Focused toward essential questions and main thrust of instruction • Specific to content/skill being taught • Formative: Ongoing throughout instruction; often informal; provides more immediate feedback; provides evidence of progress; powerful tool for achievement • Summative: Occurs at end of learning experience; includes state and standardized tests • Process: What the learner does to demonstrate skill or understanding • Authentic: Based on real-life problems or simulations
Connection	Reflect on skill of prediction/anticipation. Move focus from prediction/anticipation of skateboard to ideas that might have preceded the drive for independence and, more specifically, the colonists' decisions about how they wanted to be governed.	• A process encouraging learners' ability to recognize linkage of a completed learning engagement to the next • Ultimately encourages learners' abilities to link a completed engagement to the essential question and main thrust • Help students create a new mental model • Learning enhanced by time for reflection

1. Identify other examples of purpose, motivation, recall, engagement, assessment, and connection.

2. What support will teachers need to design these engagements?

3. How are specific engagements and essential questions related?

4. Why are connections important between the various engagements?

A key aspect of lesson plan design is the sequencing of engagements to help students answer essential question(s). Again, this involves an application of the research covered earlier in this chapter. Table 8.10 highlights the sequence of engagements. A commentary section appears alongside each of the six learning engagement components to illustrate the applications of the research on a daily basis.

Table 8.10 Sequencing of Learning Engagements for American History Part 1, Grade 7: Steps Toward Independence Unit

Learning Engagement #1 **Topic:** The New Idea **Time:** 10 minutes	Commentary
Purpose: To see how ideas are influenced by and build upon earlier ideas	Stated purpose reflects the move from a concrete example to a more abstract idea.
Motivation: Overhead image of skateboard or an actual skateboard	Student interest in a skateboard becomes the motivation for the activity.
Recall: Why do we work in groups? How are groups an integral part of discussions or cooperative learning experiences?	Recall focuses on skills involved in group work.
Engagement: In small groups, list ideas/objects/ toys/machines/past events that may have influenced the invention or development of the skateboard.	
Assessment: One person will report each group's responses. Teacher will list responses on board or newsprint. Class will indicate (by hand vote) which responses most likely influenced the invention of the skateboard.	Assessment enables the teacher to receive groups' reports and begin to move from knowledge to inference.
Connection: Reflect on skill of prediction. Move focus from prediction of skateboard to ideas that might have preceded the drive for independence and, more specifically, the colonists' decisions about how they wanted to be governed.	Connection establishes the direction for the activities to follow.
Learning Engagement #2 **Topic:** A People's Idea **Time:** 10 minutes	Commentary
Purpose: Based on available knowledge, pupils will predict factors in the drive for independence.	Skills of predicting and brainstorming are extended from engagement #1.
Motivation: Think of activities in your life that relate to being a citizen of the United States.	
Recall: What guidelines do we follow when brainstorming?	The recall continues to focus on an interpersonal skill.
Engagement: Groups predict the types of ideas that might have preceded the drive for American independence and influenced colonists' decisions about how they wanted to be governed. Write the predictions on the left side of the newsprint.	Sequencing becomes more complex as the skill becomes integrated with content.
Assessment: Informal check that all groups have created a list	Assessment is formative, moving toward the summative.
Connection: How do you think you can check to see that your predictions are correct?	Connection is an extension of the sequencing of activities. In this scenario, the connection becomes the anticipatory set for the reading activity in engagement #3.

(Continued)

Table 8.10   (Continued)

Learning Engagement #3	Commentary
Topic: Seeds of Democracy Time: 15 minutes	
Purpose: To provide students with resources and information about ideas that influenced the colonists' thinking and actions	Predictions become the purpose for reading. The newsprint format enables students to connect information learned to predictions made.
Motivation: How often are your predictions accurate?	
Recall: Review types of early colonial governments and their characteristics: colonial assembly, town meetings, and House of Burgesses.	This recall is content-oriented. Pupils are asked for a vertical recall of information learned earlier in this lesson/unit.
Engagement: Students will be given appropriate reading-level material on an aspect of English or American history. The selections include major pieces that influence the ideas held by the revolutionaries and which appear in the Declaration of Independence. Although students will read about similar topics, readings will be taken from multiple sources. Topics include Magna Carta, Enlightenment, Mayflower Compact, English Bill of Rights, Albany Plan, and Iroquois League. Students will skim reading materials to identify facts that support their predictions and write their responses in their learning journals.	Instruction is differentiated based upon reading levels and interests of students. Guided reading instruction in the content areas is crucial to successful achievement in the secondary grades. Reflection on the reading and predictions provides students an opportunity to process the content.
Assessment: After writing in learning journals, students will volunteer facts uncovered in their reading. Teacher will list facts on right side of newsprint parallel to predictions, adding new information.	In this case, teacher provides formative assessment based upon factors uncovered in the reading.
Connection: From their individual readings, students will identify words that they believe to be important.	In the connection segment, students will identify words they believe to be important in the larger context
Learning Engagement #4	Commentary
Topic: Vocabulary Development Time: 15 minutes	
Purpose: To familiarize students with the language of colonial revolutionary thinking	Purpose reflects continued chunking of subsets contained within essential question.
Motivation: As you completed the reading assignment, did you encounter words that you could not define?	
Recall: Skim the reading material again and highlight words that you could not define.	Recall provides an opportunity for skim reading and rereading for a specific purpose.
Engagement: Individually, students will list 3 words they could not define. Students will hypothesize the meaning of those words and then compare words and assumed definitions with a partner. Next, students use a dictionary to find actual meanings that best fit the context of the reading. The correct definitions will be recorded in their notebooks.	In vocabulary development, students identify words in the context of the subject matter. Although vocabulary development tends to be abstract, this learning engagement provides an opportunity to make vocabulary development concrete. Use of dictionary under supervision of social studies teacher facilitates concept development and integration of skill development with language arts.

Assessment: Teacher elicits words and definitions from each pairing of students and writes the words on the board, newsprint, or transparency	
Connection: Use of vocabulary to demonstrate understanding of a concept.	
Learning Engagement #5 **Topic:** Reflection on Essential Question **Time:** 20 minutes	**Commentary**
Purpose: To assess student depth of understanding of the idea of self-governance within English history and the colonists' ideas about freedom	Sequentially, the learning engagement provides closure to the essential question. Overall, the lesson now reflects an authentic opportunity for teaching reading and writing in the content area.
Motivation: Simulation: You are the editorial staff of a colonial newspaper and are going to create an editorial for publication.	Motivation for the learning engagement is provided by an interdisciplinary connection with the English curriculum.
Recall: What were major points raised in your reading? What were some of the key vocabulary words related to the main ideas you chose? What have you learned in your English class about writing an editorial?	Recall questions provide major readiness for the writing process.
Engagement: Individually, students will write an editorial that might have appeared in the editorial section of a colonial newspaper. In the piece, students will show how previous British or colonial events influenced the colonists' ideas about freedom. Students will include vocabulary words identified.	This engagement blends skill development, content, interdisciplinary connections, and applications to real life. The design/sequence of the learning engagement enables the student to demonstrate comprehension of the main thrust as stated in the lesson plan.
Assessment: Teacher will evaluate student writing as a draft.	The writing activity assesses the student's ability to answer the essential question.
Connection: Select one or two important statements or major points from your writing.	
Learning Engagement #6 **Topic:** Closure **Time:** 10 minutes	**Commentary**
Purpose: To connect the engagements to the main thrust of the lesson	Closure reinforces the prime-time 2 effect.
Motivation: Opportunity to read individual thoughts aloud.	
Recall: Be prepared to present the major points of your editorial.	
Engagement: Students read aloud several sentences from their editorial that show the relationship between earlier English and colonist history and the just and equal application of the law.	Students hear the connection between engagements, main thrust, and essential question. Students recognize a variety of correct interpretations that connect to the main thrust and essential question.
Assessment: Monitor students' contributions.	
Connection: In next lesson, class will participate in peer review of the editorial writing process and its historic accuracy.	

The following guide questions are provided to establish understanding of the sequence of engagements that help students answer the essential question(s):

1. How does sequencing learning engagements impact concept development?

2. How can specific learning engagements be differentiated?

3. Select one learning engagement and explain how that engagement reflects brain research, learning styles, and/or active engagement of students.

4. To what extent do the learning engagements reflect an inductive experience?

5. Explain the impact of the movement from concrete to abstract in the series of learning engagements.

SUMMARY

Many middle and high school schedules feature opportunities for extended time-period instruction on a fixed or variable basis. Research provides the classroom teacher with direction to design meaningful learning engagements, which have a positive impact on student achievement. The brain research work of Pat Wolfe, David Sousa, Robert Sylwester, Eric Jensen, and others as well as the pedagogical leadership of Robert Marzano, Heidi Hayes-Jacobs, Grant Wiggins, Jay McTighe, H. Lynn Erickson, and Carol Ann Tomlinson should be recognized and implemented on a daily basis.

Three major strategies are offered to guide this implementation process: pacing guide, unit development plan, and lesson plan prototype. This chapter defines, provides models, and serves as a resource for classroom teachers when implementing the research for effective teaching on a day-to-day basis.

A Guide for Collaborative Conversations

To set the stage for teaching in variable-length time periods and to help teachers understand the correlation of pedagogy and student achievement, the following questions serve as a guide to achieve a direct impact on curriculum and instruction:

Leader Questions

1. How do we enable teachers to see the relationship between variable-time periods and opportunities to improve student achievement?

2. On a long- and short-term basis, how do we provide teachers the opportunity to understand and implement research on teaching strategies?

3. How will the responsibility for creating and maintaining pacing guides be shared by leadership and instructional personnel?

4. How will unit development plans be implemented and updated?

5. How will a lesson plan prototype be created?

6. How will principals monitor effective teaching practices in variable-length time periods?

7. What staff development activities will prepare and support teachers as they implement effective teaching in variable-length time periods?

Teacher Questions

1. In the school schedule, what opportunities do teachers have to determine the length of the instructional periods?

2. Describe the relationship between variable-time periods and opportunities to improve student achievement.

3. How can teachers learn the current research on teaching strategies?

4. How can teachers apply the research as they teach in variable-length time periods?

5. How can teachers contribute to creating and updating pacing guides?

6. How can teachers contribute to creating and updating unit development plans?

7. How will teachers shape the lesson plan prototype for the school or district?

8. How will teachers learn to utilize the lesson plan prototype on a daily basis?

9. How will the lesson plan prototype be evaluated?

9

Implementing Change

Focused and ongoing staff development is the primary vehicle for addressing the demands of restructuring America's middle and high schools. Both educational literature and experience reveal the many initiatives that begin seeking change, reform, or restructuring but never take root. Most often the lack of permanence is due to missing ingredients: teacher input; consistent, ongoing support over time; and a clear vision of the goal. The ambiguity or perceived chaos results in resistance to the reform. The purpose of this chapter is to make connections between the research on initiatives and the applications of that research discussed in previous chapters: schedules, small learning communities, and teaching in variable-time periods.

As a part of effective change, Fullan (2000) reports the findings of Fred Newmann and Gary Wehlage (1995). They determined that high performing schools established professional learning communities. These collaborations provided professional support, involved the participants in looking at student work and assessment, and provided opportunities for teachers to work together to alter instruction to better meet student needs by using accumulated data. A collaborative community atmosphere within a school or a district veers from traditional attitudes of teacher as individual. To support the need for collaboration, Dolan decries educational communities as having encouraged the "cult of the individual" (p. 86). He suggests that overweening individualism is an element of system-in-place, the status quo, which resists onslaughts to its existence. The professional learning community challenges the status quo and involves stakeholders in meaningful work to implement change.

Due to the complexities inherent in the change process, Fullan (2000) emphasizes the lack of a "magic bullet" to expedite reform. Each school or district needs to discover the research pertinent to its needs and implement it by paving its own path and providing opportunities for local ownership of that path. Through teacher and community involvement and a focus on systemic change, possibilities exist to alter the culture of a school or district rather than simply addressing the structure—a quick, superficial, and, as a result, temporary approach to reform. A new schedule exemplifies restructuring; A focus on student learning and instructional strategies within that schedule represents a move toward reculturing.

Other aspects of the change experience include the need to think small by building change through achievable increments and to sustain progress through consistent, ongoing support and staff development. Outside influences place pressure on teachers, often to the point of saturation. In order to implement elements of change, participants in that change need to identify goals that can be reasonably accomplished. Effective leadership necessitates sensitivity to teachers' emotional and cognitive needs and demonstrates commitment to the changes for the long haul.

The "microwave society" in which we live expects change to occur immediately. Authorities on change consistently remind us that immediate change results in no change at all. In that vein, Hargreaves recommends a "slow school movement," one that takes root and ensures a more permanent change process (cited in Scherer, 2006). One major change facilitator, Michael Fullan (2000), cautions patience and consistency. Depending on the complexity of the change issues involved, change requires time and investment by those involved. He suggests a time frame of three to ten years for schools adopting various forms of change. He further promotes a dual process for change initiatives: bottom-up/top-down. This process reflects the vital role of staff development.

To ensure that the identified reforms take effect and are implemented consistently with a continuity that meets student needs, staff development planning and focus become crucial ingredients. Virginia Richardson's (2003) observations echo those of Darling-Hammond (1993) discussed earlier: For too long, teachers have been given fragmented, cafeteria-style staff development sessions that lack consistency and longevity. Although this format fails, schools persist in it for the same reasons that teachers persist in their individual approaches to change. Consequently, schools and districts need to establish a focus for staff development, allow time for it to take hold, and encourage implementation of the concepts or strategies between each session so that teachers have a basis for discussion and prior knowledge on which to build new input and understandings.

Focused staff development presents opportunities for teachers and staff members to learn about new programs, to keep current in content area practices, and to implement relevant pedagogy. By applying the research and best practices defined in the literature, teachers contribute to the restructuring of the school or district and feel ownership for the success of that venture. The authors of *Breaking Ranks in the Middle* place such importance on staff or professional development that they include it in their nine cornerstone strategies for change and improvement (NASSP, 2006). They maintain that professional development forms the basis for any ongoing commitment to change and improvement; without it, initiatives will not succeed.

In the design of professional growth sessions, the identified learning goals of the school, district, and teachers should be considered. Schools and districts need to identify their goals for improvement or reorganization and develop a master plan (Merenbloom, 1991; NASSP, 1996). Noting the lack of long-range-focused topics for staff development, Jackson and Davis (2000) cite Sparks (1998), who describes current practice in staff development as "adult pull-out programs."

Further, to begin to develop a community of learners, teachers' individual professional growth activities should fit the district's intended goals as well as their own (Jackson & Davis, 2000). In this way, a collaborative and reciprocal path benefits professional learning communities. The authors of *Breaking Ranks* (NASSP, 1996) urge each teacher to create a "Personal Learning Plan" in which learning goals, reflections, and resources are kept in a portfolio (p. 64). Without active teacher involvement, staff development may fall short in supporting instructional practice. Without classroom application and sustained follow-up, growth cannot occur.

Several authors suggest that goals for professional growth engagements include pedagogical skill as well as subject matter expertise (Bransford et al., 2000; Jackson & Davis, 2000; Marzano, 2003). Marzano cites Darling-Hammond (2000) in recognizing that a high degree of pedagogical skill enhances teacher performance and directly affects student achievement (p. 64). His comments reinforce the implementation of the pacing guide, unit development plan, and lesson plan prototype in Chapter 8, all of which provide a pedagogical structure to deliver instruction.

Staff development programs must contain opportunities for recall and connections. A single large-group staff development session fails not only the purpose of staff development but the needs of the staff involved; follow-up sessions based on the defined focus are essential (Marzano, 2003; Merenbloom, 1991; NASSP, 1996).

As teachers begin to implement the content of the staff development sessions, opportunities for conversation and feedback are provided by teams, small learning communities, and department meetings. Professional dialogue about instructional strategies or student work increases the likelihood of a more enduring learning community (Zmuda et al., 2004). The process evolves into "a personal and professional self-assessment" aimed at improvement of instructional skills and student achievement (Jackson & Davis, 2000).

The content of staff development programs arises from both administrative and teacher input. The input presented in this book relies on the interrelationship between change theory and staff development practice. This interrelationship has a major impact on three major aspects of school reform: scheduling, small learning communities, and teaching in variable time periods.

Rather than suggesting separate leader and teacher questions, as at the end of Chapters 1–8, this closing chapter offers the following universal recommendations, which should be discussed at the district, school, small learning community, and department levels:

1. Define the reasons for and obstacles to change.

2. Advocate for sthe needs of students to drive the reorganization effort.

3. Provide training for implementing research related to restructuring secondary education.

4. Involve teachers in a collaborative decision-making process.

5. Accept anxiety and uncertainty as developmental aspects of the change process.

6. Support teachers' efforts to function in a positive, trusting, and safe environment.

7. Plan opportunities for teachers to select and assess their personal goals as well as the goals of the team, small learning community, department, school, or district.

8. Recognize the schedule and instructional components within the schedule as means to an end, not ends unto themselves.

9. Include formative and summative assessment of the reorganization endeavor.

10. Embed a curriculum component in the restructuring process.

11. Craft staff development engagements to be active and hands-on.

12. Implement shared leadership between administrators and teachers to provide a balance between top-down and bottom-up initiatives.

13. Motivate teachers to add new dimensions to the program by recognizing that change involves the addition of new skills through practice and feedback.

Making Creative Schedules Work in Middle and High Schools reflects the concepts of patterns and relationships. Structural options are based on patterns that allow individual schools and districts to adopt the options that best fit their allocated time. The relationships between scheduling possibilities and instructional uses of time provide a basis for an in-depth look at teams or small learning communities and how they meet the needs of students. Questions at the end of each chapter lead the reader to answer the broader, essential question of how to implement reorganization plans that serve students.

From one perspective, *Making Creative Schedules Work in Middle and High Schools* provides a microcosm of organizational models and concrete examples: restructuring, scheduling, establishing small learning communities, and preparing teachers to teach effectively in variable-time periods. Simultaneously, a macrocosm view includes a more global or holistic perspective: Teachers and leaders work collaboratively to address the relationships among the needs of students, the organization of the school, and provisions for improving student achievement. Ideally, the reader will recognize and implement both perspectives.

References

Allen, J. (2004). *Tools for teaching content literacy.* Portland, ME: Stenhouse.

Allen, R. (2002). Big schools: The way we are. *Educational Leadership, 59*(5), 36–41.

Alspaugh, J. W. (1998). Achievement loss associated with the transition to middle school and high school. *Journal of Educational Research, 92*(1). Retrieved January 28, 2005, from HighBeam Research Web site: http://www.highbeam.com/library/

Ames, N. (2004). Lessons learned from comprehensive school reform models. In S. C. Thompson (Ed.), *Reforming middle level education: Considerations for policymakers* (pp. 131–154). Greenwich, CT: Information Age.

Anfara, V. A., Jr. (2001). Setting the stage: An introduction to middle level education. In V. A. Anfara, Jr. (Ed.), *The handbook of research in middle level education* (pp. vii–xx). Greenwich, CT: Information Age.

Anfara, V. A., Jr., & Brown, K. M. (2001). Advisor-advisee programs: Community building in a state of affective disorder? In V. A. Anfara, Jr. (Ed), *The handbook of research in middle level education* (pp. 3–34). Greenwich, CT: Information Age.

Arhar, J. M. (2003). No Child Left Behind and middle level education: A look at research, policy, and practice. *Middle School Journal. 34*(5), 46–51.

Arhar, J. M., Johnston, J. H., & Markle, G. C. (1992a). The effects of teaming and collaborative arrangements. In J. H. Lounsbury (Ed.), *Connecting the curriculum through interdisciplinary instruction* (pp. 15–21). Columbus, OH: National Middle School Association.

Arhar, J. M., Johnston, J. H., & Markle, G. C. (1992b). The effects of teaming on students. In John H. Lounsbury (Ed.), *Connecting the curriculum through interdisciplinary instruction* (pp. 23–30). Columbus, OH: National Middle School Association.

Arnold, J., & Stevenson, C. (1998). *Teachers' teaming handbook.* New York: Harcourt Brace.

Beers, K. (2003). *When kids can't read: What teachers can do: A guide for teachers 6–12.* Portsmouth, NH: Heinemann.

Biancarosa, G., & Snow, C. E. (2004). *Reading next: A vision for action and research in middle and high school literacy.* Washington, DC: Alliance for Excellent Education.

Biehler, R. L. (1974). *Psychology applied to teaching.* Boston: Houghton Mifflin.

Blum, R. W. (2005). A case for school connectedness. *Educational Leadership, 62*(7), 16–20.

Bransford, J., Brown, A. L., & Cocking, R. R. (Eds.). (2000). *How people learn: Brain, mind, experience, and school* (Expanded ed.). Washington, DC: National Academy Press.

Brown, D. F. (2001). Flexible scheduling and young adolescent development. In V. A. Anfara, Jr. (Ed.), *The handbook of research in middle level education* (pp. 125–139). Greenwich, CT: Information Age.

Brown, K. M. (2001). Get the big picture of teaming: Eliminate isolation and competition through focus, leadership, and professional development. In V. A. Anfara, Jr. (Ed.), *The handbook of research in middle level education* (pp. 35–71). Greenwich, CT: Information Age.

Burkhardt, R. M. (2001). Advisory: Advocacy for every student. In T. O. Erb (Ed.), *This we believe and now we must act* (pp. 35–41). Westerville, OH: National Middle School Association.

Campbell, L., Campbell, B., & Dickinson, D. (1996). *Teaching and learning through multiple intelligences* (2nd ed.). Boston: Allyn & Bacon.

Capelluti, J. & Brazee, E. (2003). Teaming at the middle level: Promising practice or unfulfilled promise? *Principal Leadership* (Middle School Ed.) *3*(5), 32–37.

Cavaretta, J. (1998). Parents are a school's best friend. *Educational Leadership, 55*(8), 12–15.

Closing achievement gaps. (2004). *Educational Leadership, 62*(3).

Copland, M. A. & Boatright, E. E. (2004). Leading small: Eight lessons for leaders in transforming large comprehensive high schools. *Phi Delta Kappan, 85*(10), 762–770.

Danielson, C., & McGreal, T. L. (2000). *Teacher evaluation to enhance professional practice.* Alexandria, VA: Association for Supervision and Curriculum Development.

Darling-Hammond, L. (1993). Reframing the school reform agenda: Developing capacity for school transformation. *Phi Delta Kappan, 74*(10), 752–761. Retrieved on February 2, 2005, from HighBeam Research Web site: http://www.highbeam.com/library/

Darling-Hammond, L. (1995). Restructuring schools for student success. *Daedalus 124.* Retrieved February 2, 2005, from HighBeam Research Web site: http://www.highbeam.com/library/

Davies, M. A. (1992). Are interdisciplinary units worthwhile? Ask students. In J. H. Lounsbury (Ed.), *Connecting the curriculum through interdisciplinary instruction* (pp. 37–41). Columbus, OH: National Middle School Association.

Davis, G. A. (2001). Point to point: *Turning points* to *Turning points 2000.* In V. A. Anfara, Jr. (Ed.), *The handbook of research in middle level education* (pp. 215–239). Greenwich, CT: Information Age.

Doda, N. (1992). Teaming: Its burdens and its blessings. In J. H. Lounsbury (Ed.), *Connecting the curriculum through interdisciplinary instruction* (pp. 45–55). Columbus, OH: National Middle School Association.

Dolan, W. P. (1994). *Restructuring our schools: A primer on systemic change.* Kansas City, MO: Systems & Organization.

Downes, A. (2001). It's all in the family: Middle schools share the secrets of parent engagement. *Middle Ground* 4(3), 9–15.

Erb, T. O., (1992). What team organization can do for teachers. In John H. Lounsbury (Ed.), *Connecting the curriculum through interdisciplinary instruction* (pp. 7–14). Columbus, OH: National Middle School Association.

Erb, T. O. & Stevenson, C. (1999). From faith to facts: Turning Points in action—What difference does teaming make? *Middle School Journal, 30*(3), 47–50.

Erickson, H. L. (2001). *Stirring the head, heart, and soul: Redefining curriculum and instruction* (2nd ed.). Thousand Oaks, CA: Corwin Press.

Erickson, H. L. (2004). Foreword. In H. H. Jacobs (Ed.), *Getting results with curriculum mapping* (pp. v–ix). Alexandria, VA: Association of Supervision and Curriculum Development.

Faber, S. H. (2004). *How to teach reading when you're not a reading teacher.* Nashville, TN: Incentive.

Falk, B. (2002). Standards-based reforms: Problems and possibilities. *Phi Delta Kappan, 83*(8). Retrieved February 2, 2005, from HighBeam Research Web site: http://highbeam.com/library/

Felner, R. D., Jackson, A. W., Kasak, D., Mulhall, P., Brand, S., & Flowers, N. (1997). The impact of school reform for the middle years: Longitudinal study of a network engaged in Turning Points-based comprehensive school transformation. *Phi Delta Kappan, 78*(7), 528–550.

Fogarty, R., & Stoehr, J. (1995). *Integrating curricula with multiple intelligences.* Thousand Oaks, CA: Corwin Press.

Fullan, M. (2000). The three stories of educational reform. *Phi Delta Kappan, 81*(8), 581–584. Retrieved October 31, 2005, from Phi Delta Kappan Web site: http://www.pdkintl.org/kappan/kappan.htm

George, P. S., & Alexander, W. A. (1993). *The exemplary middle school* (2nd ed.). New York: Harcourt Brace.

Hackmann, D. G. (2002). Block scheduling for the middle level: A cautionary tale about the best features of secondary school models. *Middle School Journal, 33*(4), 22–28.

Hackmann, D. G., Petzko, V. N., Valentine, J. W., Clarks, D. C., Nori, J. R., & Lucas, S. E. (2002). Beyond interdisciplinary teaming: Findings and implications of the NASSP national middle level study. *NASSP Bulletin, 86,* 33–47.

Hayes-Jacobs, H. (1997). *Mapping the big picture: Integrating curriculum & assessment K-12.* Alexandria, VA: Association of Supervision and Curriculum Development.

Hayes-Jacobs, H. (Ed.). (2004). *Getting results with curriculum mapping.* Alexandria, VA: Association for Supervision and Curriculum Development.

Hines, R. A. (2001). *Inclusion in middle school* [Electronic version]. Retrieved March 2, 2005, from University of Illinois Clearinghouse on Early Education and Parenting Web site: http://ceep.crc.uiuc.edu/

Holloway, J. H. (2001). Research Link: Inclusion and students with learning disabilities. *Educational Leadership, 58*(6) 86–88. Retrieved March 2, 2005, from Association of Supervision and Curriculum Web site: http://www.ascd.org/

Jackson, A. W., & Davis, G. A. (2000). *Turning points 2000: Educating adolescents in the 21st century.* New York: Teachers College Press.

Jensen, E. (1998a). *Introduction to brain-compatible learning.* Thousand Oaks, CA: Corwin Press.

Jensen, E. (1998b). *Teaching with the brain in mind.* Alexandria, VA: Association for Supervision and Curriculum Development.

Kagan, S. (1994). *Cooperative learning.* San Clemente, CA: Kagan.

Kasak, D. (2001). Flexible organizational structures. In T. O. Erb (Ed.), *This we believe . . . and now we must act* (pp. 90–97). Westerville, OH: National Middle School Association.

Kohn, A. (2003). Almost there but not quite. *Educational Leadership, 60* (6), 27–29.

Lambert, L. (2005). Leadership for lasting reform. *Educational Leadership. 62*(5), 62–65.

Lipsitz, J., Mizell, H. H., Jackson, A. W., & Austin, L. (1997). Speaking with one voice. *Phi Delta Kappan, 78*(7), 533–540.

Marzano, R. J. (2003). *What works in schools: Translating research into action.* Alexandria, VA: Association for Supervision and Curriculum Development.

Marzano, R. J., Pickering, D. J., & Pollock, J. E. (2001). *Classroom instruction that works: Research-based strategies for increasing student achievement.* Alexandria, VA: Association for Supervision and Curriculum Development.

McAdams, R. P. (1997). A systems approach to school reform: Five factors that affect school reform. *Phi Delta Kappan, 79*(2). Retrieved January 28, 2005, from HighBeam Research Web site: http://www.highbeam.com/library/

McEwin, C. K., Dickinson, T. S., & Jenkins, D. M. (2003). *America's middle schools in the new century: Status and progress.* Westerville, OH: National Middle School Association.

McEwin, C. K., Dickinson, T. S. & Smith, T. W. (2004). The role of teacher preparation, licensure, and retention in creating high-performing middle schools. In S. C. Thompson (Ed.), *Reforming middle level education: Considerations for policymakers* (pp. 109–129). Greenwich, CT: Information Age.

McTighe, J., & Wiggins, G. (1998). *Understanding by design handbook.* Alexandria, VA: Association for Supervision and Curriculum Development.

Merenbloom, E. Y. (1991). *The team process: A handbook for teachers* (3rd ed.). Columbus, OH: National Middle School Association.

Mulhall, P. F., Flowers, N., & Mertens, S. B. (2002). Understanding indicators related to academic performance. *Middle School Journal, 34*(2) 56–61. Retrieved June 3, 2006, from NMSA Web site: http://www.nmsa.org/Publications/MiddleSchool%20 Journal/November2002/article10/tabid/421/Default.aspx

National Association of Secondary School Principals. (1996). *Breaking ranks: Changing an American institution.* Reston, VA: Author.

National Association of Secondary School Principals. (2004). *Breaking ranks II: Strategies for leading high school reform.* Reston, VA: Author.

National Association of Secondary School Principals. (2006). *Breaking ranks in the middle.* Reston, VA: Author.

National Council of Teachers of English, National Council of Teachers of Mathematics, National Council for the Social Studies, National Science Teachers Association, & International Reading Association. (2005). *Standards for middle and high school literacy coaches and subject matter teachers* (Draft). Retrieved on April 5, 2005, from National Council of Teachers of English Web site: http://www.ncte.org/collec tions/literacycoach

National Middle School Association. (1995). *This we believe: Developmentally responsive middle level schools.* Columbus, OH: Author.

Noguera, P. A. (2004). Transforming high schools. *Educational Leadership, 61*(8), 26–31.

Norton, J. (2000). An interview with Anthony Jackson: Turning Points 2000 and the future of middle-grades reform. *Phi Delta Kappan, 81*(10). Retrieved March 5, 2005, from HighBeam Research Web site: http://www.highbeam.com/library/

Nussbaum, D. (2004, September 12). Why middle schools are being questioned. *New York Times.* Retrieved October 13, 2004, from MiddleWeb Web site: http://www .middleweb.com/mw/news/NYTmstroubles.html

Richardson, Virginia. (2003). The dilemmas of professional development. *Phi Delta Kappan, 84*(5), 401–406. Retrieved May 24, 2006, from Phi Delta Kappan International Web site: http://www.pdkintl.org/kappan/k0301ric.htm

Scherer, Marge. (2006). The challenge to change. *Educational Leadership, 63*(8), 7.

Schurr, S., Lewis, S., LaMorte, K., & Shewey, K. (1996). *Signaling student success: Thematic learning stations and integrated units.* Alexandria, VA: National Middle School Association.

Schurr, S., & Lounsbury, J. (2001). *Revitalizing teaming to improve student learning* (Staff Development Kit #3). Westerville, OH: National Middle School Association.

Senge, P. M. (1990). *The fifth discipline: The art & practice of the learning organization.* New York: Doubleday.

Senge, P. M., Cambron-McCabe, N., Lucas, T., Smith, B., Dutton, J., & Kleiner, A. (2000). *Schools that learn: A fifth discipline fieldbook for educators, parents, and everyone who cares about education.* New York: Doubleday.

Sousa, D. A. (2006). *How the brain learns* (3rd ed.). Thousand Oaks, CA: Corwin Press.

Stevenson, C. (1998). *Teaching ten to fourteen year olds* (2nd ed.). New York: Longman.

Stiggins, R. J. (2001). *Student-involved classroom assessment* (3rd ed.). Upper Saddle River, NJ: Merrill Prentice Hall.

Stronge, J. H. (2002). *Qualities of effective teachers.* Alexandria, VA: Association for Supervision and Curriculum Development.

Sylwester, R. (1995). *A celebration of neurons: An educator's guide to the human brain.* Alexandria, VA: Association for Supervision and Curriculum Development.

Task Force on Education of Young Adolescents. (1989). *Turning points: Preparing American youth for the 21st century.* Washington, DC: Carnegie Council on Adolescent Development.

Tomlinson, C.A. (1999). *The differentiated classroom: Responding to the needs of all learners.* Alexandria, VA: Association for Supervision and Curriculum Development.

Tomlinson, C. A., & Doubet, K. (2005). Reach them to teach them. *Educational leadership, 62*(7), 9–15.

Trimble, S. (2003). Research-based classroom practices and student achievement. In J. L. Irvin (Ed.), What research says. *Middle School Journal, 35*(1), 52–58.

Vars, G. (2001). Can curriculum integration survive in an era of high stakes testing? *Middle School Journal, 33*(2), 7–17.

Wang, M. C., & Reynolds, M. C. (1997). Progressive inclusion: Meeting new challenges in special education. *LSS Publication Series (3).* Retrieved March 2, 2005, from Association of Supervision and Curriculum Association Web site: http://ascd.org

Wheelock, A. (1998). *Safe to be smart: Building a culture for standards-based reform in the middle grades.* Columbus, OH: National Middle School Association.

Wiggins, G., & McTighe, J. (1998). *Understanding by design.* Alexandria, VA: Association for Supervision and Curriculum Development.

Williams, R. B., & Dunn, S. E. (2000). *Brain-compatible learning for the block.* Thousand Oaks, CA: Corwin Press.

Williamson, R. D., & Johnston, J. H. (1998). The fate of middle schooling. *The School Administrator, 55*(7) (Web edition), 30–33. Retrieved March 2, 2005, from American Association of School Administrators Web site: http://www.aasa.org

Williamson, R. D., & Johnston, J. H. (2004). Creating academically challenging middle level schools. In S. C. Thompson (Ed.), *Reforming middle level education: Considerations for policymakers* (pp. 33–48). Greenwich, CT: Information Age.

Wolfe, P. (2001). *Brain matters: Translating research into classroom practice.* Alexandria, VA: Association for Supervision and Curriculum Development.

Yecke, C. P. (2006, February 1). Mayhem in the middle [Commentary]. *Education Week, 44.*

Zmuda, A., Kuklis, R., & Kline, E. (2004). *Transforming schools: Creating a culture of continuous improvement.* Alexandria, VA: Association for Supervision and Curriculum Development.

Index

CORWIN PRESS

The Corwin Press logo—a raven striding across an open book—represents the union of courage and learning. Corwin Press is committed to improving education for all learners by publishing books and other professional development resources for those serving the field of PreK–12 education. By providing practical, hands-on materials, Corwin Press continues to carry out the promise of its motto: **"Helping Educators Do Their Work Better."**